S0-AAB-668

Paddling Yellowstone and **Grand Teton** National Parks

Don Nelson

FALCON®

HELENA, MONTANA

A FALCON GUIDE®

Falcon® Publishing is continually expanding its list of recreational guidebooks. All books include detailed descriptions, accurate maps, and all the information necessary for enjoyable trips. You can order extra copies of this book and get information and prices for other Falcon® guidebooks by writing Falcon, P.O. Box 1718, Helena, MT 59624, or calling toll-free 1-800-582-2665. Also, please ask for a free copy of our current catalog. Visit our website at www.falconguide.com.

© 1999 by Falcon® Publishing, Inc., Helena, Montana.
Printed in the United States of America.

2 3 4 5 6 7 8 9 0 MG 04 03 02 01 00

Falcon and FalconGuide are registered trademarks of Falcon® Publishing, Inc.

All rights reserved, including the right to reproduce this book or parts thereof in any form, except for inclusion of brief quotations in a review.

Cover photo by Jon Gnass.
All black-and-white photos by the author unless otherwise noted.

Library of Congress Cataloging-in-Publication Data

Nelson, Don, 1948–
    Paddling Yellowstone and Grand Teton national parks / Don Nelson.
        p.   cm. —
    Includes index.
    ISBN 1-56044-627-7 (pbk. : alk. paper)
    1. Kayak touring—Yellowstone National Park—Guidebooks. 2. Canoes and canoeing—Yellowstone National Park—Guidebooks. 3. Kayak touring—Grand Teton National Park (Wyo.)—Guidebooks. 4. Canoes and canoeing—Grand Teton National Park (Wyo.)—Guidebooks. 5. Yellowstone National Park—Guidebooks. 6. Grand Teton National Park (Wyo.)—Guidebooks. I. Title.
    GV776.Y45 N45   1998
    917.87'520443—ddc21   98-47217
                                                                          CIP

CAUTION

Outdoor recreational activities are by their very nature potentially hazardous. All participants in such activities must assume responsibility for their own actions and safety. The information contained in this guidebook cannot replace sound judgment and good decision-making skills, which help reduce risk exposure, nor does the scope of this book allow for disclosure of all the potential hazards and risks involved in such activities.

Learn as much as possible about the outdoor recreational activities in which you participate, prepare for the unexpected, and be cautious. The reward will be a safer and more enjoyable experience.

 Text pages printed on recycled paper.

To my son, Jesse, whose life adds
immeasurably to mine

Contents

Multi-day trips

Shoshone Lake

Yellowstone Lake

7. PADDLING TRIPS IN GRAND TETON NATIONAL PARK

Day trips

Jackson Lake

Snake River

Multi-day trips

Acknowledgments

If the act of writing a book is a rather private activity—a solo trip, in a sense—it certainly takes place in a landscape created by many human streams and tributaries, each contributing to and influencing the character and evolution of the landscape in which the book evolves.

The tributaries that have influenced my "stream of consciousness" are many. I want to especially thank Jim Newman, my "other dad," who gave me important outdoor experiences early in my life when it mattered a lot. Thanks to the entire Newman clan for what they have given me throughout the years.

Thanks need to go to my own son, Jesse, my paddling companion, pal, and "compass bearing" when my boat seemed a bit small in a big, rough sea. Thanks, too, to his mom, Mardy, for the times of messing around in little boats, and the time and money to build some along the way.

The staff and the board of the Yellowstone Association supported me during my years in Yellowstone, allowing me an enormously important experience in a wonderful place, and indirectly, but literally, making this book possible.

My thanks to the Central Backcountry Office of Yellowstone National Park and to Dan Burdette and Janet Wilts of Grand Teton National Park for their time and effort spent in reviewing relevant parts of the manuscript for accuracy and completeness. I very much appreciate their contribution.

Thanks to Mike, Rob, and the crew at Vic's Espresso and News in Boulder, Colorado, for graciously allowing me to take up space while writing for many, many hours. They make the best espresso drinks in the West, to which I have become thoroughly addicted.

Special thanks, too, to Bill Schneider of Falcon Publishing for planting the seed, and to my editors, Ric Bourie and Arik Ohnstad, also of Falcon, for their patience and guidance.

And finally, thanks to all those I have laughed and cried with around the campfire, especially Michael Bartley, Dave Butler, Mike Eisenstat, Jim Guenther, John King, and the Nelson gang.

I am indebted to each of you.

Map Legend

US Highway	
Paved Road	
Unimproved Road	
Parking Area	
Lake, River/Creek,	
Marsh or Wetland	
Trail	
Boat Launch	
Optimal Crossing Route	

City or Town	Gardiner
Campground	8Q7 Moose Creek
Cabin or Building	
Peak	Mt. Moran
Park/Refuge/Forest Boundary	
Map Orientation	N
Scale	0 0.5 1 Miles

Map of Yellowstone and Grand Teton National Parks

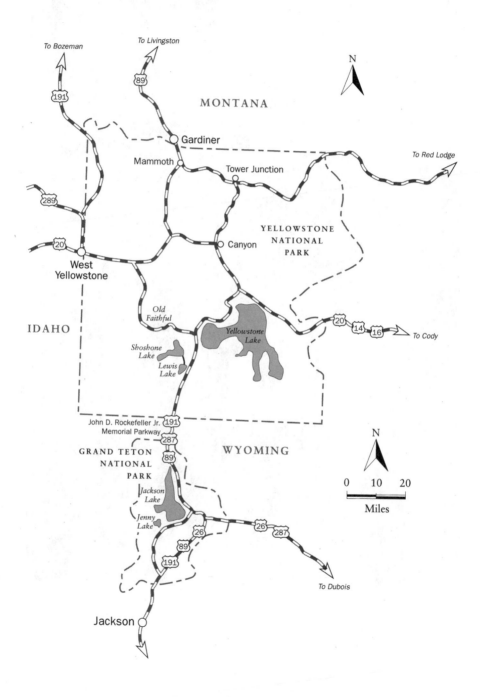

Jesse Nelson, the author's son, paddles his kayak across Jenny Lake.

Introduction

In the northwest corner of Wyoming is a cluster of lakes, large and small, that were created by violent volcanic activity and the slow carving of glaciers. These lakes lie within the boundaries of Yellowstone and Grand Teton national parks. They also lie within one of the most unique natural places and one of the largest, nearly intact temperate-zone ecosystems remaining in the world: the Greater Yellowstone ecosystem.

The two national parks—beautiful, vast, and wild—are the heart of this ecosystem. To dip a paddle into a lake at Yellowstone or Grand Teton national park, to paddle for part of a day or a week in the backcountry, is to explore this heart by immersing yourself in its wildness, where the Earth's natural processes and cycles are today very much as they have been for millennia. Paddling these lakes in a canoe or touring kayak is the focus of this guide.

As busy a place as Yellowstone Park can be at times, only 3 or 4 percent of its 2.2 million acres is considered developed land, that is, it has been altered by humans into roads and fairly civilized amenities, such as motels, restaurants, and visitor centers. The rest of the park, the vast majority of the land, is pristine backcountry traveled by a relatively small portion of the park's visitors, and it is a backcountry that is eminently reachable. Though Grand Teton National Park is smaller, the same can be said of its backcountry. Wild places can always be reached, and relatively easily, by those willing to take the time to travel under their own power. When the backcountry is bordered by water, paddling is one of the best ways to get there.

The lakes of Yellowstone and Grand Teton national parks are large enough for extended overnight trips, where a good dose of wilderness is assured. At the same time, a novice paddler who prepares properly can explore a small part of one of the lakes for a few hours with the kids and do so safely. The variety of paddling opportunities also allows for relaxed days on the water, where you can leisurely explore the shore or go fishing before returning to your camp or motel at day's end. For the more experienced, there are longer trips to take and more strenuous open-water conditions to tackle, offering greater challenge as you paddle your way to a remote backcountry camp.

Yellowstone Lake is a very large and very cold lake—the largest freshwater lake in the United States above 7,000 feet. With a surface area of 136 square miles and with 110 miles of shoreline to explore, you can paddle for many days and come back again and again to experience its many moods. The three arms of the lake, located on the southern side, have dozens of shoreline campsites for the backcountry traveler. Because of its size, its location, and park management policies, you can be assured of finding the remoteness, seclusion, and challenge you seek in a wilderness experience.

Just to the southwest of Yellowstone Lake lie Lewis and Shoshone lakes. Both are excellent choices for a backcountry trip. Lewis Lake, with its boat launch and adjacent campground, is a favorite among anglers and presents opportunities to look for bird life or moose or to pause at its shoreline thermal basin. Shoshone Lake, the most popular destination in Yellowstone for backcountry paddlers, offers a wide diversity of shoreline campsites and enough wilderness for great multi-day trips. Visiting the wild and undeveloped Shoshone Geyser Basin on the lake's western shoreline is a must when you travel into this paradise of backcountry paddling.

Connecting Lewis and Shoshone lakes is the 3.5-mile long Lewis River Channel, the only river in Yellowstone Park on which visitors may paddle. It winds, sometimes quickly, downstream from Shoshone Lake, passing around sandbars, fallen trees, lily pads, rock outcrops, and the occasional small hot spring.

To the south of Yellowstone National Park is the smaller, but vastly beautiful and rugged Grand Teton National Park. With the snow-covered Teton Range as a backdrop, you can easily reach by vehicle a series of glacially carved lakes in the park. From their eastern shores, a canoe or kayak can also transport you to some of the rugged trails this park is known for. The largest of these lakes, Jackson Lake, covers approximately 40 square miles with a shoreline that measures 70 miles. The northern end is particularly remote. The southern end has several islands worth exploring. Immediately to the south of Jackson Lake is a series of smaller lakes—Leigh, Jenny, and String lakes—which can provide a secluded, serene experience, even in the middle of the summer. The Snake River winds through Grand Teton National Park and provides excellent, often exciting floating for intermediate paddlers who are comfortable negotiating rapidly moving water with frequent obstacles. While there is no camping along the Snake River in the park, excellent day paddling can be found for most experience levels.

The two parks abound in natural and human history. With every mile of shoreline explored, the backdrop is a vast, wild landscape which supports the largest populations of elk and bison in North America and some of the largest populations of grizzly bears and wolves in the contiguous United States. The mountain peaks that surround the parks' waters are the result of massive uplifts and widespread volcanic eruptions, and have been sculpted by long periods of glacial activity. The hundreds of streams that flow out of the hills and mountains are clear and cold. They and the lakes they flow into are considered to be some of the finest fisheries in the lower 48 states.

These lakes and rivers offer astounding natural beauty and a variety of challenges as their temperaments change throughout the day. They demand respect, not only for their pristine natural state, but for their tendency, especially in the case of the lakes, to turn wind-whipped and forbidding in an instant. Given the respect they deserve, these waters offer experiences that can be found nowhere else in the United States. Peaceful campsites and private beaches, exciting trout fishing, and days of solitude are all very available to the self-propelled adventurer.

Wildland safety warrants a chapter of its own, but it should be noted early on that no matter what kind of paddling experience you are seeking, you have this guarantee: Regardless of lake size, water temperatures are always very cold, and surface conditions do change rapidly. On bodies of water the size of Yellowstone, Shoshone, and Jackson lakes, a true "big lake" experience should be anticipated. Large waves of 2 to 3 feet or more can develop quickly during the buildup of afternoon wind. During storms, waves as high as 5 to 6 feet are not uncommon. Combine large waves with water temperatures in the 40s to 50s, and you have conditions that are hazardous, if not life threatening, especially if your boat should capsize. Do not ignore these very real possibilities, but don't let them keep you from some of the most enjoyable paddling in the Rocky Mountain West. Anticipate the risks and plan ahead for possible emergencies.

In the pages that follow, you'll find information to help plan and carry out a paddling adventure into the Yellowstone-Teton backcountry that is appropriate for you, that is safe, and that treats the landscape responsibly. Enjoy this water wilderness.

USING THIS GUIDEBOOK

This book is organized into three main parts. The first part, Chapters 1 through 5, serves as an introduction and trip-planning section. The second and third parts each describe specific paddling trips in Yellowstone National Park (Chapter 6) and Grand Teton National Park (Chapter 7). The first chapters are designed to help you get oriented and organized in preparation for a safe journey. The trip descriptions in the Yellowstone and Grand Teton sections will help you grasp the diversity of paddling experiences that await you.

Chapter 1, Safety on the water and in the wilderness, contains important information to help you understand, and deal with, the physical risks of paddling a big lake, the region's frequently fickle weather, and the possibility of encountering Yellowstone's bears and other wildlife, especially when camping. We have placed this chapter close to the front of the book because it should be one of the first you read. Please don't overlook it in your eagerness to get to other parts of the book. Paddling the lakes of Yellowstone and Grand Teton or paddling on the Snake River can be a joy, especially when the weather and conditions are calm. We include a good deal of information about paddling under less-than-ideal conditions because when wind and weather conspire to make paddling more challenging, the inherent danger of paddling these waters grows.

Do not let these warnings frighten you away from paddling in the parks. At the same time, be prepared and know how to avoid dangerous winds and waves.

Chapter 2, The region past and present, provides a brief look at the natural and cultural histories of the Yellowstone and Grand Teton areas. Many of the trip descriptions include more details on these subjects.

Chapter 3, Permits and regulations, includes a brief but important orientation to the topic, and information on the various permits that may be required. With regard to Backcountry Use Permits, and a full understanding of the complex procedure required to obtain a permit and itinerary for an overnight paddling trip in either park, it's best to contact the park directly for more detailed information. We have chosen to provide a cursory explanation because of space limitations.

Chapter 4, Backcountry ethics and etiquette, gives extensive ideas on how to minimize your impact on the land and waters you'll be visiting, a practice increasingly termed Leave No Trace. In addition to advice on how to keep the wilderness wild, you'll find some suggestions on wilderness manners.

Chapter 5, The outfit, is meant to help you gather the appropriate boats, equipment, clothing, and food you'll need to travel comfortably and safely in the wilderness. The chapter ends with a checklist that can be used to prepare for your trip.

The heart of this guidebook, the trip descriptions, provides detailed, practical information on 20 paddling trips in Yellowstone National Park and 18 trips in Grand Teton National Park. These include day trips and multi-day trips. The routes and itineraries are meant as informative suggestions. The details therein can also be used to design trips of your own choosing. Remember, though, that itineraries for overnight trips will be dictated by which campsites you are assigned on your Backcountry Use Permit. For details, see Chapter 3, Permits and Regulations.

Each description is organized by the following headings:

Character is a brief summary of the trip—where it goes and the features that make the trip worth including in this book.

Total paddling distance gives the water miles you will travel. Of course, the route you take may differ based on wind and other factors. One of the pleasures of paddling is that there are no true paths to follow—no roads, junctions, or interchanges laid out on the surface of the water. Set a course and go.

Average paddling time is included for day trips. This, too, is an approximation, subject to the abilities and whims of each paddler, and very dependent on how often you stop for rests or relief.

Suggested time is offered for longer trips, in an attempt to provide a time consistent with the trip's difficulty rating.

Put-in and **take-out** are sometimes different but more often the same. Most of the trips in this book are round trips. Launch points are marked on the book's maps to help in planning your trip.

Difficulty offers a subjective rating according to the challenges of each trip and is meant to help match your paddling and backcountry skills with an itinerary appropriate for you and your party. The ratings are based primarily on paddling mileage, general water conditions, and to some degree, on the distances of open-water crossings. Any paddling experience can become dangerous with the strong winds, high waves, and cold water common to this area. Reading Chapter 5, Safety, is a must to gain an accurate understanding of the paddling risks and their assessment.

Ratings are inherently relative and are to be used only as general guidelines. Some feel that there are no "easy" trips on the lakes of this area, and this may very well be true. The rating—easy, moderate, or difficult— should, at the very least, give you a sense of relative differences between various trips. An easy rating should never be interpreted as casual or of no risk. Remember when choosing an itinerary that a party is only as strong as its least able paddler. Approach any trip itinerary conservatively, using your past experiences, physical strength, and stamina as a guide to your planning. Always consider and plan for rapid weather changes and severe conditions. Start and finish early in the day to avoid the buildup of afternoon wind while you are on the water. If you have any questions or concerns, contact a ranger before embarking on your trip.

Easy trips are shorter, more leisurely, shoreline paddles reasonably comfortable for people new to paddling or wilderness travel. **Moderate** trips involve longer mileages, potentially rougher water, and may have at least some open-water crossings. People who have had at least some paddling experiences on which to assess their capabilities may be comfortable with trips of this rating. **Difficult** trips involve the longest paddling mileage and have longer open-water crossings, and more of them. Only people who are in good physical condition and who have considerable paddling experience and a lot of stamina should attempt these trips.

Campsites that are listed in the multi-day trip descriptions represent the ideal points to stop for the day. Don't expect to get each and every campsite you want when you request a Backcountry Use Permit, as mentioned above. If these sites are not available when you get your permit, check the maps for alternative sites. Most backcountry sites can be reserved ahead of time by phone or in person. Your itinerary of reserved sites is then converted to a Backcountry Use Permit, in person, once you arrive at the respective park. For details, see page 22.

Be aware of lists potential hazards or simple precautions to consider in your travel. As repeated elsewhere, these are not intended to alarm you, but simply to help you prepare adequately for backcountry travel. Few trips on the waters of Yellowstone or Grand Teton national parks result in accident or tragedy. In the interest of keeping it that way, these considerations are mentioned.

Attractions gives a few points of interest along the route or opportunities (bird watching or fishing, for example) that the trip presents.

Maps are essential for navigating the waters of the parks. The maps included in this book are designed to give you a general idea of trip routes, campsites, and interesting features along the way. They are meant to be used for trip planning, not as navigational tools. We strongly urge readers who plan a trip to acquire the maps listed in this section. Most are published by the United States Geological Survey (USGS). Other helpful maps that show larger areas are published by each park and by Trails Illustrated and Earthwalk Press. See the Appendix for phone numbers and addresses of these publishers.

Use is another subjective rating. Compared to other parts of the United States, where large populations are trying to use limited waterways, you'll find the waters of the Yellowstone-Teton area relatively free of congestion. Because of park management and backcountry use restrictions, it is uncommon to encounter many other paddlers. Therefore, most trips have a light or moderate use rating, but remember that these are very busy parks, and you will be encountering concentrations of people at certain times and places.

Directions tell how to get to the put-in points. Both parks are relatively easy to drive in. Between these directions and the maps, you should have no trouble finding your way.

The paddling is the narrative description of the route and what you are likely to discover along the way.

The book's Appendix helps in planning your trip by providing addresses and phone numbers of offices in both parks that you'll need to contact for further information and for required permits. In addition, the addresses and phone numbers of map publishers are included.

1. Safety on the Water and in the Wilderness

Once you push off from shore and begin to paddle across the clear waters of the larger lakes of the area—Yellowstone, Jackson, Lewis, and Shoshone—you enter a place of beauty, thrills, and adventure, but more importantly, a place of risks. Understanding those risks and continually assessing them will help keep you off the list of those who have experienced serious mishaps or death on these waters. This said, it must also be noted that wilderness travel can sometimes bring adversity into your outdoor living experience; if you want to avoid adversity entirely, stay at home.

Throughout the following chapters of this book, you'll find specially noted advice on how to stay safe. These recommendations are flagged for the reader in boldface as **a word to the wise**.

ASSESSING THE RISKS AND PREVENTING ACCIDENTS

When you paddle on the "big lakes" of the Yellowstone-Teton area, do so with awareness, anticipation, and deliberateness. These lakes have many moods and their waters are exceedingly cold, particularly in Yellowstone where water temperatures range from 43 to 55 degrees in the summer. To keep your travels free of disaster, you'd do well to heed the following guidelines:

1. Always wear a life jacket or personal flotation device whenever you are in a boat on the waters of Yellowstone and Grand Teton national parks. Don't let calm waters or sunny weather convince you otherwise. The temperature of the water beneath your boat should be enough to convince you of the need for a life jacket in the event you should fall in.
2. Be acutely aware of the weather around you and to any changes that may be taking place.
3. Always paddle near enough to shore so you can land quickly and safely when lake conditions become too challenging. Your distance from shore should depend on weather, water conditions, and your skill level, especially if you are traveling solo. Use good sense, anticipate possible problems, and don't take chances.
4. In general, lake crossings are not recommended; shoreline travel is strongly preferred by park personnel. However, in certain situations short crossings may be called for and will be described in the trip itineraries. Before any crossing is attempted, be extremely cautious in your assessment of current water conditions, and look to the sky for changing weather conditions, especially in the direction of prevailing winds.

The buildup of a thunderstorm over Yellowstone Lake can be common on summer afternoons.

5. Take your time and wait out stormy conditions in a safe place rather than putting yourself at risk by adhering to what may have become an unsafe itinerary.

6. When paddling in a group, always remember that you can travel only as far and as fast as the least capable member of your party. Plan your itinerary and adjust your paddling to accommodate this reality. Paddling together is not only the safest way to travel, it's good for camaraderie.

7. Before departing on your trip, whatever its length, have a plan of action in the event of a serious mishap such as an injury, illness, or a capsized boat. Keep in mind that capsizing rarely happens in calm conditions, but rather in physically demanding situations that can complicate rescue attempts, especially when you are weary after a long day of paddling in rough weather. Before the trip, consult a good canoeing or kayaking manual and practice rescuing a capsized boat in the nearest available lake, pond, or pool with the members of your traveling party.

8. Remember that while park rangers are highly trained to assist you in the event of an emergency, realistically speaking, you are on your own. Help is a long way off in almost all situations. Don't expect or count on it.

9. At the risk of repeating myself: Under any lake conditions, ALWAYS adjust your paddling pace and distance from shore to accommodate the range of experience and ability in your party. Both solo paddlers and groups increase their risks when they are too goal-oriented or destination-bound. Relax and enjoy the paddling experience and diversity of your group. Stick together! Plan and carry out your trip with a pace that does not fatigue paddlers to the point that the journey is no longer fun. An overachieving pace puts all of you at risk if water conditions become more challenging or a mishap occurs.

WEATHER AND LAKE CONDITIONS

Winter stays late in the Yellowstone-Teton country. Ice cover typically does not break up until late May or early June, and the Lewis-Shoshone Lake area often has ice until the second or third week in June. (If you are planning an early season trip, consult the specific park for current paddling conditions.) During the summer, Yellowstone National Park, at a higher elevation than Grand Teton, has slightly cooler temperatures and more precipitation.

Always be aware that mountain weather can change quickly and may result in cold temperatures, freezing rain, sleet, and even snow throughout the summer months. Strong, gusty afternoon winds are common and can be accompanied by large waves, rain, and lightning. (On lakes in Grand Teton National Park, strong winds commonly flow down canyons, changing the lake conditions very quickly, especially near the canyon mouth.) Avoid lake crossings, even short ones, during the midafternoon. If lightning occurs, get off the water and away from the lakeshore. Thick forests of equal height offer the best protection in these conditions.

Average temperature and rainfall, June through September

	June	July	August	September
YELLOWSTONE NATIONAL PARK				
Average high temperature (degrees Fahrenheit)	68	75	76	69
Average low temperature (degrees Fahrenheit)	36	39	37	29
Average rainfall (inches):	2.1	1.9	1.1	1.1
GRAND TETON NATIONAL PARK				
Average high temperature (degrees Fahrenheit)	71	81	79	69
Average low temperature (degrees Fahrenheit)	37	41	39	32
Average rainfall (inches):	2	1	1	1

Two important things to always keep in mind when paddling in this area are water temperature and wave size. Water temperatures are cold, usually no warmer than the 50s even in midsummer, and will be debilitating in the event of a soaking. The longer you are wet, the greater your chances of hypothermia or death. Even 10 to 15 minutes of immersion in the cold waters of the area will leave you hypothermic. You must simply avoid at all costs going into the water accidentally, and if you do, have a well understood plan to get you, or a member of your party, out of the water as quickly as possible.

The changing surface is what makes paddling an otherwise flat lake interesting, but wind, and the waves that result, can be fatiguing and can dump you into the water if you are not careful. Large waves are not just the result of stormy weather either. Afternoon winds, even on beautiful sunny days, are a common occurrence and can easily create waves of 2 to 3 feet in height. Waves of 5 to 6 feet are not uncommon. Waves of this size can wear out even the strongest paddler and can easily swamp or capsize a canoe or kayak if you are not skilled or using great care. Pace yourself and stay very close to shore when it's windy and the waters are choppy. Always carry a large sponge and bailer or bilge pump in each craft.

If you capsize, stay with your boat and have a plan of action ready to implement. As emphasized above, don't wait until you're on your trip, on the water, or in the water to develop the plan. If another boat in your party upsets, assist them as quickly as possible and get to shore to assess the situation.

Plan to adjust your paddling day to avoid the predictable high wind and waves in the afternoon. If lake conditions become too challenging for the abilities of anyone in your group and you have not arrived at your destination, travel close to shore or hold up on shore until wind and waves subside. It is better to arrive late than totally beleaguered or not at all.

HYPOTHERMIA

Hypothermia, known more simply as exposure, is the lowering of the body's core temperature, and the risk of hypothermia is inherent in paddling any of Yellowstone's or Grand Teton's waters. If not treated, it can result in death. Cool or cold conditions, accompanied by wetness and wind, contribute to the loss of body heat. Capsizing a canoe or kayak will, of course, result in the likelihood of serious heat loss and possible hypothermia, but rain or a cold wind blowing across the water, especially in conjunction with fatigue, can also begin to chill the body dramatically.

Signs and symptoms of hypothermia can include apathy, lethargy, disorientation, incoherence, confusion, shivering, and clumsiness. When weather conditions are conducive to hypothermia, avoid it by staying dry, protecting yourself from wind, and by wearing additional layers of clothing. When packing your gear each day, always pack your rain gear and extra clothes where you can get to them quickly and easily, no matter how hot and sunny conditions may be. Easy access is essential. Of course, keeping them dry is no less important. Pack these essentials in a dry, waterproof bag.

If a member of your party becomes hypothermic, or prehypothermic, prevent any further heat loss by removing the person from the cold conditions. If paddlers get wet, get them out of their wet clothes and into dry ones, including a warm hat and gloves. Keep them out of the wind. Insulate their head and neck, and prepare a warm beverage for them to drink.

DEHYDRATION

The Yellowstone-Teton area is, in general, a dry climate. If you are from a more humid environment, you'll notice that perspiration is not as evident here as at home. Physically active people, including paddlers, are often unaware they are

Water, water everywhere but don't forget to drink.

losing body fluids as fast they are. Additionally, synthetic fabrics that are intended to wick moisture away from the body often give you the sense that sweating is not taking place when it actually is. Thirst is not always an indicator either, and by the time you do feel thirsty, your body is already getting dehydrated.

Dehydration is a serious problem because it can lead to a loss of strength, an impairment of concentration and coordination, and general fatigue. It affects a paddler's health, safety, and performance. Replenishing body fluids will prevent or reverse these negative effects. The key is to drink before you feel thirsty or feel other indications of dehydration and to drink often and drink more than you may think you need.

While paddling, keep drinking water nearby and easily accessible.

BEARS AND BUGS

The Yellowstone-Teton area is bear country and bug country. Both critters are present in varying numbers and at different times, and dealing with them takes awareness and adjustments in attitude and approach. Neither, however, should be a reason not to explore the region's waters and backcountry.

Mosquitoes, and occasionally flies, are about the only biting insects occurring in numbers that can be a nuisance. Their numbers are unpredictable so come prepared with a good insect repellent, and give them fewer areas to feed on by using a head net and covering exposed skin with long sleeves and pants. Their presence is hard to ignore; just don't let them keep you from enjoying your surroundings. Whether we like it or not, they are a part of the natural landscape.

Dealing with bears is far more serious than dealing with biting insects. Both black and grizzly bears are common in the Yellowstone-Teton area. They are clear symbols of the wildness that exists here, and their presence is a reassurance that not every landscape has been civilized to their exclusion. Park management policies protect the bear and help with human and bear coexistence. Therefore, some human activity is restricted in certain places at certain times to better assure the bear's success. Park information handouts will tell you specifically which areas are closed and when. These dates may vary somewhat from year to year, but generally speaking, mid-July is the latest that bears cause travel restrictions for paddlers.

Camping in bear country can conjure up fears of mythological proportions, and while a degree of fear is healthy, actual risk of a bear encounter is exceedingly low. You can also take precautions to further reduce the chance of such an encounter. Numerous books are available to help you better understand bear behavior and how to adjust your own behavior to avoid bears. When you register for a backcountry permit in either park, you will receive valuable information on this topic. Read it and implement it. For your safety and that of the bear, do not ignore it!

As rare as close encounters with bears are, they can be made virtually nonexistent by not doing four things:

Hang all food and bear attractants high from the bear pole provided at most campsites.

1. Do not surprise a bear.
2. Do not get near a bear and her cubs.
3. Do not get too close to a bear with food.
4. Do not attract bears to your campsite.

Stay alert at all times and to avoid surprising a bear, make noise in places where long-range visibility is poor, such as walking over a hill or around a bend in a trail through thick vegetation. Since you will be traveling by water, and not necessarily hiking down trails, your chance of a bear encounter will come when you are in and around camp. You can minimize your chances by:

- Leaving foods with strong odors at home
- Not eating or storing food in your tent
- Hanging your food and garbage at least 10 feet above the ground and 4 feet or more from the nearest tree trunk
- Hanging with your food all scented personal products such as deodorant, toothpaste, sun screen, and lip balm
- Keeping a clean camp and sleeping, when possible, at least 100 yards from where you cooked and stored your food
- Not sleeping in the clothes you cooked in

If you do encounter a bear in camp, stay calm. Never run, and only climb a tree if you can get at least 15 feet above the ground and can do so well before the bear is near, an unlikely event. If a bear enters camp in the day, back away slowly, avoiding direct eye contact. With a bear in camp at night, be aggressive, defend yourself, make lots of noise, and do not play dead.

For more extensive advice on how to avoid bears and how to handle encounters, *Bear Aware* by Bill Schneider (Falcon Publishing, 1996) is an excellent book.

Lastly, a word about bear repellent sprays: They are not a substitute for alertness, for avoiding bear confrontations, or for taking the proper precautions to avoid bears. Do not let yourself become cocky and overconfident. Remember that repellent sprays have a short range and can be greatly affected by wind and rain. Some authorities recommend the use of repellent sprays, some do not. If you choose to use a spray, keep it handy and available, especially in your tent at night.

A FINAL LOOK AT THE USE OF CAUTION

The vast majority of paddlers are careful and use caution when they head out onto the waters of Yellowstone and Teton national parks. Yet each year people run into serious problems and, every so often, death results. In almost every case, upon further analysis, serious mishaps and deaths were usually preventable.

Yellowstone National Park archivist Lee Whittlesey's fascinating book, *Death in Yellowstone* (1995), describes the more serious accidents that have occurred on

Yellowstone's three large lakes and presents a sobering look at the dangers inherent in the cold, and sometimes rough, waters of the region. For example: Over the years, at least four people have drowned on Shoshone Lake. In 1958, a 32-year-old man drowned after the boat he and a companion were paddling was swamped by 5-foot waves and capsized. Cold water prevented a rescue by the survivor, and the victim's body was never recovered in the 200-foot-deep water.

In 1978, while crossing Shoshone Lake, a fierce windstorm resulted in the drowning of two Boy Scouts. Waves 4 to 5 feet high created havoc, capsizing boats and immersing several boys and leaders in 45-degree water. With hypothermia setting in and conditions worsening, their survival was at risk. Other paddlers came to the rescue. Nonetheless, two scouts—the oldest and strongest—died. The combination of open water, rapidly changing weather conditions, improperly loaded canoes, and a group spreading out too far to be able to assist each other, all contributed to the tragedy.

In 1994, a 22-year-old park ranger on routine patrol drowned when 3- to 4-foot waves and a 35-mile-per-hour wind capsized his sea kayak. He struggled to get back into his boat but eventually succumbed to hypothermia.

Lewis Lake, though smaller than Shoshone Lake, has also seen its share of tragedies, where at least seven people have drowned. Sudden storms with strong winds and large waves, combined with the very cold waters and less-than-sound judgment on the part of paddlers, have figured in the equation and resulted in death for inexperienced and experienced boaters alike.

As you might imagine, Yellowstone Lake has seen the most deaths over the years. More than 40 people have drowned on its waters, including two very experienced men during the summer of 1997. It is probably safe to say that all of these people headed out for an enjoyable day on the waters of Yellowstone Lake before tragedy struck. As elsewhere throughout the two parks, sudden high winds, 3- to 6-foot waves, and frigid waters all combined to create high-risk situations.

Recounting the story of deaths on the large lakes of Yellowstone is not intended to scare you into staying away from the many beautiful paddling adventures that await you in the Yellowstone-Teton area. Instead, these sad stories are intended to instill a healthy respect for the realities that exist in big lake paddling and to encourage you to use wisdom and good sense so that you have the fun and memorable experience you set out to have.

2. The Region Past and Present

NATURAL HISTORY

The Yellowstone-Teton area is located roughly halfway between the equator and the North Pole. Its landscape is the result of extraordinary geologic activity, driven at least in part by a major plume of molten rock rising from the Earth's core. Millions of years of volcanic activity and a fracturing of the Earth's crust are the result of the forces exerted by heat rising from the molten plume.

Grand Teton National Park is a vertical park. Its world-renowned mountains—true skyscrapers formed long before metal or glass existed—epitomize the Rockies. For 5 million years, the Rockies have been rising along a fracture, or fault, running north-south in the Earth's crust. As they have done so, very hard rock, 3 billion years old, has been exposed to the extremes of changing climates. Over thousands of years, ice has formed and melted, carving and reshaping this rock into what we see today—one of the grandest mountain scenes on the planet.

At the base of this mountain landscape, and just to the east, are the cluster of clear, cold, glacially carved lakes described in the Grand Teton chapter of this guide.

Yellowstone National Park, while just to the north, is a very different place than the Teton area. Nearly surrounded by mountains, its origins are primarily volcanic, and its bubbling, steaming thermal features are dramatic evidence of the molten plume's current activity. While Yellowstone's geologic history dates back 4

Mount Moran and its canyon are formed partly of the 3-million year old rock in Grand Teton National Park.

billion years, most of the physical landscape witnessed today is the result of massive volcanic episodes taking place about 50 million years ago, followed by a more recent eruption of enormous scale and proportion which shook and flowed over the landscape about 600,000 years ago. This most recent eruption resulted from the bursting of a 30- by 45-mile area of the earth's crust that had been swelling and bulging over the plume. Its burst released an enormous volume of volcanic material, enough to cover thousands of square miles with ash flows, molten rocks, and lava creating much of what exists today: a high plateau largely surrounded by mountains. Evidence of the Yellowstone Caldera, a large dishlike depression left by the explosion, while not easy to see, nonetheless exists. Subsequent lava flows, years of glacial activity, and erosion have rendered the caldera less impressive than it once was, but immediately south of Dunraven Pass, which is north of Canyon Village, roadside turnoffs give you a view of the northern part of the caldera. On Yellowstone Lake, the south rim of the caldera cuts across the north edge of the Promontory, and along Flat Mountain Arm. The high bluffs near Madison Junction, north of the Madison River, show part of the caldera's north rim.

As in the landscape of the Tetons, glacial activity as recent as 10,000 to 12,000 years ago imparted the final sculpting of the Yellowstone landscape that you see today. The two major lake areas in Yellowstone are situated in, or very near, the Yellowstone Caldera.

In the Yellowstone-Grand Teton area, flora and fauna evolved to inhabit the surface of the landscape left lifeless by the volcanic action, the upthrusting, and the glaciation. These plants and animals have experienced many changes over time, evolving in tropical and subtropical climates. Today the Greater Yellowstone ecosystem is an area largely covered by a variety of cone-bearing trees and grassy meadows, teeming with communities of animals, birds, fish, and other diverse creatures.

Plant life responds directly to the temperature, amounts of moisture, soil type, and wind of its surroundings. Based on these four physical factors, the approximately 1,700 or so different plants in the Greater Yellowstone area can be grouped into zones based on elevation. Within those zones, the plants can be grouped further into major plant communities. Zones range from the dry and relatively warm lower elevations, where grasses and sagebrush thrive, to the highest locations, where only low lying alpine plants can survive. Between these extremes a variety of conifer forests dominate the landscape, with Douglas-fir, lodgepole pine, Engelmann spruce, and subalpine fir covering the mountainsides from lower to higher elevations and in roughly that order. Other trees, including aspen, cottonwood, juniper, and limber and whitebark pines are mixed throughout the system. Some areas, because of various physical factors, will favor grasses over trees. These meadow areas can be found at all elevations.

When you paddle the lakes and rivers of the Yellowstone-Teton area, you can view most of the plant zones and communities, depending on the elevation of the body of water you are on. Since, however, your travels will be associated with water, you can expect to spend most of your time near the plant communities that enjoy water as much as you do.

The plant community most common along these shores is the riparian community, that narrow band of vegetation between the aquatic community and the drier uplands. The dominant plants in this transition area include cottonwood, aspen, Douglas-fir, willow, water birch, alder, and occasional blue spruce trees, cattails, mosses, grasses, and water lilies.

While the riparian community comprises only about 1 percent of the landscape, about three-fourths of the region's wildlife depends on it for their survival. Wildlife of all kinds come through this community on their way to the water and as they move between high and low elevations. The woody plants, such as willow, are attractive forage plants for deer, elk, and moose. Many small birds nest in the riparian areas or spend time there feeding on insects that are attracted to the moisture. Small mammals find safety and raise their young in the relatively dense vegetation. Muskrats and beaver depend on the water for safety and for food. The taller trees, such as cottonwood and spruce, become nesting and perching places for eagles and ospreys that depend on fish for food.

Living within the waters of the Yellowstone-Teton area are 21 species of fish. The fisheries of the area are known by humans worldwide for their health and productivity, but many other creatures also depend on this resource. Bald eagles, ospreys, loons, mergansers, and pelicans feed on fish from spring through fall. It is claimed that pelicans alone consume more than 300,000 pounds of trout from Yellowstone Lake! Grizzly bears feed on spawning cutthroat trout through June and into July. The trout provide a major source of protein for the bears.

The source of all this water is the snow that accumulates to great depths throughout the winter in the mountains of the Greater Yellowstone area. During the short summer months, the snow cover melts and retreats to the highest elevations where permanent snow fields remain.

CULTURAL HISTORY

There is evidence of humans inhabiting the Greater Yellowstone area for at least 10,000 years, more than likely moving in as the climate warmed with the closing of the most recent Ice Age. These early nomadic hunters sought the region's large mammals. Many of those animals are now extinct, but sheep, deer, elk, moose, and bear remain.

Early people, organized into tribes and living in the Great Plains, moved into what would become the Greater Yellowstone area in the late eighteenth and early nineteenth centuries. Evidence of their presence exists throughout the landscape where they wandered, tapping into the "food and fiber" resources both within the current-day parks and on the plains to the east.

When paddling the waters described in this guide, think of the early foraging people resting along the same shorelines you use today. They were there, pausing for a while, perhaps also reflecting on what they were doing or on their own humanness, as they searched the landscape for sustenance.

When Lewis and Clark touched briefly on the northern edges of the Greater Yellowstone area in the early nineteenth century, they ushered in the coming of the whites. Their reports and those of the trappers to follow stimulated a growing interest in the region, leading to government-funded explorations organized to further validate the sometimes fantastic impressions of the area. The scientists and artists of these expeditions did indeed validate the uniqueness and beauty, fantastic or not, held within the entire Yellowstone-Teton area, and within a short time the world's first national park, Yellowstone, was established, soon to be followed by the creation of Grand Teton National Park.

The establishment of the first national park, and future parks for that matter, is taken for granted by most people, but it was really quite a remarkable event—remarkable because the very concept of the park idea meant that we humans would be expected to voluntarily behave differently within the park borders, an amazing expectation in 1872, when development and settling of the West, with all its altering and subduing, was being encouraged by every institution we had.

That members of our species, the Washington-based political establishment, were able to hold up a hand in a gesture of restraint, saying, in essence, "enough is enough," is truly remarkable and reason for continued hope.

When a paddler moves silently across the lakes or rivers of Yellowstone or Grand Teton national park, there is so much more to it than just paddling. There is the twofold benefit the soul gets out of directly experiencing ecological quality and integrity, while doing so in a setting that is a direct reflection of what the human spirit is capable of.

A reflective morning on the South Arm of Yellowstone Lake.

3. Permits and Regulations

Millions of visitors come each year to enjoy Yellowstone and Grand Teton national parks. This many visitors can have an impact on the natural resources of the area, so the National Park Service, in an effort to balance human use with the protection of the natural resources, imposes limits on several activities through the issuance of permits. Issuing permits also provides the park with the opportunity to educate the public about minimizing impact on the land and about safe recreation. Permits, therefore, in addition to a park entrance fee, are required to use your boat, to fish, and to camp in the parks' backcountry. By being prepared for the costs and the possible limitations imposed by the permits, you can clearly and efficiently plan your paddling experience.

Park entrance fees

While fee increases are always possible, Yellowstone and Grand Teton national parks currently charge a $20 entrance fee per vehicle, allowing travel within both parks for a seven-day period. The fee is collected at any park entrance station. You can purchase an annual Golden Eagle pass for $50 that allows entrance into all national parks throughout the country. There are also discounts that apply for senior citizens.

Boat use, permits, and fees

A permit is required in both parks for boat use. For nonmotorized, hand-propelled craft, the fee is currently $5 for a seven-day permit or $10 for an annual permit. These fees are always susceptible to increases.

When you purchase a boat permit, park personnel will walk you through a safety and equipment checklist. Remember: In both parks, anyone in a watercraft must **wear** a U.S. Coast Guard-approved personal flotation device (PFD) at all times.

In **Yellowstone National Park**, nonmotorized, hand-propelled boating is allowed on all park lakes except for Sylvan Lake, Eleanor Lake, Twin Lakes, and Beach Springs Lagoon. As mentioned earlier, Yellowstone, Lewis, and Shoshone lakes are the most easily accessed. To protect the water resources, wildlife, and views of the landscape, no boats of any kind, including fishing float tubes, are permitted on rivers or streams, with the exception of the Lewis River Channel between Shoshone Lake and Lewis Lake.

While the use of motorized craft and sailboats are permitted on most of Yellowstone Lake, water skiing and jet skis are not. In the two southern arms of the lake, motorized boats are restricted to 5 miles per hour, and the extreme southern ends of all three arms are limited to hand-propelled craft only.

In Yellowstone National Park, permits for nonmotorized boats can be obtained at the South Entrance Station, Lewis Lake Ranger Station, Grant Village

Boating zones on Yellowstone Lake

Visitor Center, Bridge Bay Marina, Lake Ranger Station, and the Canyon and Mammoth visitor centers.

In Grand Teton National Park, Jackson Lake and four nearby smaller lakes—Leigh, String, Jenny, and Two Ocean—offer a range of paddling experiences. All but Leigh Lake are easily accessed by vehicle. Though not covered in this guide, nonmotorized boats are also permitted on Phelps, Emma Matilda, Taggart, Bradley, and Bearpaw lakes. Permits can obtained at the Moose or Colter Bay visitor centers.

Jackson Lake is a large lake nearly 17 miles long and up to 9 miles wide, with about 70 miles of shoreline. Motorboats, jet skis, sailboats, and sailboards are

Kayaks at rest on the Lewis River Channel.

allowed on Jackson Lake, but because of its large size, conflicts with hand-propelled craft can be minimized or avoided completely. Motorized boats under 8 horsepower are permitted on Jenny Lake.

Backcountry camping permits and reservations

Both parks require Backcountry Use Permits for all overnight use. The permits designate which campsites you'll occupy for each night you are in the backcountry. Both parks have backcountry sites accessible by boat, a limited number of which may be reserved in advance by mail or in person or, at Grand Teton, by fax. Neither park accepts reservations for Backcountry Use Permits by phone.

At this writing, a nonrefundable $15 fee was being charged for advance reservations, but fees may go up at any time. If you are successful at reserving a site, you'll receive a written confirmation. If a site you requested is not available, you will be notified of other available sites. The confirmation must then be converted to the actual Backcountry Use Permit *in person*, no more than 48 hours in advance of your first camping date in Yellowstone, no more than 24 hours in advance in Grand Teton. If you do not pick up your permit before 10:00 A.M. on the day of your trip or confirm the reservation by phone, your site(s) will be made available to others. For Yellowstone National Park, reservations are strongly recommended.

For Yellowstone National Park, reservations will be accepted *only* by mail or in person at a ranger station no earlier than April 1. The Backcountry Use Permit may be picked up at a ranger station in the park or at the Central Backcountry Office at the Albright Visitor Center in Mammoth Hot Springs.

Reservations for Backcountry Use Permits for Grand Teton National Park can be made by mail, fax, or in person (at the Moose Visitor Center) from January 1 to May 15. Write to the park's permit office, listed in the Appendix. After May 15, reservations must be made in person at the Moose Visitor Center within 24 hours of your departure. Permits may be picked up at both the Moose and Colter Bay visitor centers or at the Jenny Lake Ranger Station. For details on how to receive Grand Teton's "Backcountry Camping" brochure, see details in the Appendix.

If you have not reserved a site, any remaining unreserved sites may be obtained when you arrive in Yellowstone or Grand Teton. You can do this up to 48 hours before your first camping date in Yellowstone or up to 24 hours before your first camping date in Grand Teton.

There are numerous lakeshore sites located on Shoshone Lake and Yellowstone Lake. All sites are limited to no more than eight people. Heavy use of campfires in this area over the years has resulted in undesirable impacts in and around campsites. In an effort to repair past damage, Shoshone Lake is now a "no wood fire" area. Stoves or charcoal are the only sources for heat and cooking permitted.

Both lake areas in Yellowstone are an important resource to both human and wildlife populations. As elsewhere in the park, the needs of wildlife are given a priority. This is particularly true for the bear populations around Yellowstone Lake that feed on the cutthroat trout that spawn by the thousands in more than 100 small streams that enter the lake. To minimize possible conflicts with bears, many of the three dozen campsites available to boaters either restrict travel away from the camp or remain closed until mid-July. There are other use restrictions as well.

For a complete and detailed description of backcountry use of Yellowstone National Park, including all policies, procedures, and campsite locations, consult the "Backcountry Trip Planner," available by calling or writing the park. For details, see the Appendix.

The Brimstone Point campsite on the Southeast Arm of Yellowstone Lake.

In Grand Teton National Park, lakeshore campsites are located on Jackson and Leigh lakes. Jackson Lake has 15 total sites, 5 of which are group sites designated for 7 to 12 people. All other sites are limited to 6 people. Leigh Lake, limited to nonmotorized boats, has 6 backcountry sites, one of which is designated for group use.

Fishing permits and licenses

Fishing seasons, locations, catching methods and techniques, and "catch and release" requirements are regulated and enforced. Please read and follow specific park regulations throughout your fishing.

In **Yellowstone National Park**, anyone 16 years of age or older is required to purchase a fishing permit. At this writing, a ten-day permit cost $10 and annual permits cost $20. Individuals 12 to 15 years of age are required to obtain a nonfee permit. State fishing licenses are not a substitute for a Yellowstone fishing permit. Permits can be obtained at all ranger stations, visitor centers, and Hamilton General Stores.

In **Grand Teton National Park**, a Wyoming state fishing license is required and can be obtained in the park at the Moose Village Store, Signal Mountain Lodge, Colter Bay Marina, and Flagg Ranch Village.

4. Backcountry Ethics and Etiquette

When you are considering a paddling experience into the backcountry of a place as special and unique as the Yellowstone-Teton area, you may want to explore several philosophical and practical topics. Two of those are: What is wilderness and is the Greater Yellowstone area a true wilderness? and, Should we conduct ourselves differently in this place, and if so, how?

The first topic is important because if the Greater Yellowstone area is a wilderness, or has wilderness attributes, then you can expect to experience conditions unique to a wild place. The latter topic is especially interesting because if this is a wilderness, how we conduct ourselves may have to be altered, voluntarily or otherwise, in order to have an experience without compromising the attributes of wilderness that attracted us in the first place.

How we should conduct ourselves in wilderness settings is something that is continually evolving because, first of all, there is an ever-diminishing amount of wilderness and an ever-increasing number of people wanting to use it, and secondly, the philosophy of how we define what is right and wrong changes. Let's take a look at these topics.

IS THE GREATER YELLOWSTONE AREA A TRUE WILDERNESS?

A definition of true wilderness is a tough one to agree on. Certainly part of the definition includes size. Is the place big enough to "feel like" wilderness? Can you get away from the sights and sounds of humanity and its developments? Can you find seclusion and a sense of remoteness? Is there an opportunity for physical challenge and self-reliance?

Certainly the Greater Yellowstone area has many of these characteristics of wilderness. The Greater Yellowstone ecosystem, roughly the size of the state of Maine, is indeed a big place. Yellowstone National Park alone contains more than 2 million acres, most of which are as wild as they were when the park was set aside in 1872. As big and wild as the area is, it's being encroached upon by civilization. It is, out of protective necessity, a highly managed place. Because of the highly managed nature of the area, some would say that this area is not a true wilderness, but remember: While visitors to this place *are* highly managed, the natural systems are not. Ironically, because of the intense management, a wilderness experience can, without question, be had here.

If you can look beyond the managed aspect of the place, accepting as a trade-off all its inherent control over human behavior, you can still immerse yourself day after day in something very close to a true wilderness.

Predators of all sizes still hunt their prey here as they have since primeval times. Bison and elk still roam by the thousands throughout the landscape as the seasons come and go. And the great winter snows still feed the streams, and the streams the lakes, and the waters are still clear and relatively pure. The rich human

It's almost always apparent where you should pitch your tent and where you should prepare meals at a designated campsite.

history of the region is still with us, but there are more humans than ever before coming to this place we call Yellowstone Country. We have to be aware of the impact our numbers can have and adjust our behavior so that a wilderness experience can be had by each of us, today *and* tomorrow.

LEAVE NO TRACE

When they issue permits to travel and camp in the Yellowstone-Teton backcountry, park rangers also give brief lessons that will help you understand how to travel lightly, minimizing your impacts as you go. If there is a "code of conduct" for traveling in the Yellowstone-Teton area, it is one that demonstrates *respect* for the land. If the concept of respect is understood, we can minimize our impacts.

The skills and habits necessary can be summarized by the following concepts:

Plan ahead and prepare. When you plan ahead, you then know what regulations exist for the specific area you will be visiting so your expectations will be met. Planning your menu and repackaging your food into reusable containers helps you minimize food waste while reducing trash and litter in the backcountry. Choosing the right equipment helps you minimize both your impact and your visibility to others. For example, a small stove eliminates the impact of cutting or gathering wood, and earth-colored clothes and shelters blend in with the surroundings better than bright colors.

Camp and travel on durable surfaces. Concentrate your activities in areas that show signs of previous use, and reduce your impact on more delicate, easily damaged places. In the designated campsites, it's apparent where tents have been pitched and where meals have been prepared; do as those who've come before you. When it's time for rest stops, choose sand beaches or bedrock rather than muddy or vegetated areas. When hiking, stay on designated trails and don't shortcut the switchbacks.

Pack it in and pack it out. Leave a clean landscape wherever you go, and properly dispose of what cannot be packed out. Pick up all trash, garbage, and spilled foods in camp and along the way. Do not bury any food scraps or trash or dispose of it in pit toilets. Too many people use the campsites to make this an acceptable practice, and animals may be attracted to your camp and will often dig up what you buried and scatter it around.

In areas without pit toilets, solid human waste should be deposited in small holes (catholes), dug 6 to 8 inches deep, in an inconspicuous place at least 100 feet from water, camp, or trails. Fill the hole with the loose soil and replace the sod or duff as you found it, leaving the site disguised with natural materials. Use toilet paper sparingly and burn it, where fires are allowed, or pack it out. Do not bury it in the cathole; it decomposes very slowly.

Urine does not need to be buried, but keep it well away from camp and water supplies.

Some campsites include pit toilets; at others, it's necessary to bury human waste.

When washing dishes or yourself, avoid or at least minimize the use of soap. Wastewater should be scattered at least 100 feet away from camp and water sources. Remove food particles from the water before disposing of it and pack them out with other litter, or burn them in your fire, if one is permitted.

There are differing opinions as to the best way to dispose of fish guts and other remains. Some feel they should never be put back into the stream or lake since decomposition occurs slowly in the cold water of the area and it is highly unlikely that they will be consumed by other animals. These people feel that the remains should be buried in a cathole, several hundred yards downwind from your camp. Since fish remains attract bears, however, park regulations ask you to puncture the air bladder and dispose of all entrails in deep water.

If a fire is permitted where you are camping, you may burn paper, leftover food and garbage, and cans; but before leaving, sift through the ashes to remove any unburned cans, food scraps, and foil. Then pack it out.

Just before departing the site, scout the entire area to make sure you've removed all indications of human visitors. Whether it's yours or a previous visitor's, you'll do the park a favor by picking up anything nature has not deposited.

Leave what you find where you found it. You may come across some natural artifact in the backcountry that holds special meaning to you, a "souvenir" reminder of the wonderful experience you've had. Resist the temptation to remove it. Unless it's trash, leave what you find where you found it.

Removal of any item from the park is not only against the law, but it deprives other visitors of the same sense of discovery you experienced. This goes for picking flowers and other plants and moving rocks and logs. Leave no trace by leaving things where you find them. It's as simple as that.

Use fire minimally and responsibly. Ironically, one of the greatest pleasures and one of the greatest *impacts* in the backcountry comes from campfires. Though campfires occasionally spark wildfires, the greatest impacts come from the damage done to both living and dead trees by firewood gatherers, the unsightly fire rings full of large half-burned logs, and the compaction of soil around the ring.

Because of the impacts, wood fires in the backcountry are discouraged and in some places prohibited. Portable stoves are recommended for cooking. In areas where wood fires are permitted they should be kept small, using small sticks and branches from trees that are dead *and* down. Leave your saws and axes at home. They are not necessary for the wood that should fuel your fire. While gathering firewood, spread your impact over a wide area well away from camp. Branches should not be cut or broken off any standing tree, even if the tree is dead.

Always use the existing fire ring. Despite the impact you'll have on the area, this is preferable to building additional rings.

If you build a campfire, remember that it must be attended to at all times, cleaned up and extinguished completely when you leave camp.

Better yet, next time you're in the backcountry, try sitting around a couple of candles instead of a campfire. It's not as warm and not as bright, but you might be surprised at how satisfying it can be.

WILDLAND ETIQUETTE

These last few items relate to things somewhat more subtle and less tangible, but nonetheless important. They are born out of the same concept of respect for the landscape, but in this case they have more to do with respect for other backcountry travelers.

The Greater Yellowstone ecosystem has lots of elbow room for free-roaming animals to carry on their lives as they have for hundreds of centuries. In relatively recent times, humans have "suddenly" appeared in their habitats, and in increasing numbers. Because of use restrictions, human numbers are limited in the backcountry, but human behavior is left pretty much up to self-enforcement. Respect the needs of the other animals using the wilderness backcountry. Paddlers need to be especially aware of birds that are attracted to lake and river areas to feed, nest, and raise their young. Bald eagles and ospreys, two birds common to the waters of the area, are extremely sensitive to human disturbance. Keep your distance, and if you find yourself in a nesting area, leave immediately to avoid further disturbance.

Some birds that are attracted to lakes are colonial nesters, usually using island sites to protect themselves and their young from predators. Pelicans, cormorants, and terns are colonial nesters of the area. To avoid disturbing them, keep well offshore, at least a quarter mile, in areas where these birds are nesting. Nesting birds are protected by law. Contact rangers ahead of time if you have any questions about locations or your potential impacts.

Paddlers also spend time in the habitat of bears, especially until mid-July while spawning trout are a primary food source. This is particularly true on Yellowstone Lake. Closures are in effect at various times and places to allow bears to feed undisturbed. The trip descriptions in this book refer to seasonal closures, but carefully read all park materials you receive when you reserve a backcountry campsite.

Remember that there are "human animals" out there, too. Keeping your group small makes traveling easier and enables other groups to also achieve the wilderness experience. Respect other visitors' need for solitude by traveling quietly and minimizing disturbances as you go from place to place. Shouts and other noises carry easily across water and can diminish the wilderness experience for others. Leave radios and CD/tape players at home. Let the sounds of nature prevail. There is nothing worse than hearing someone else's music interfering with the sound of a loon and your own solitude.

Watercourses and portages can occasionally get congested with other boats and paddlers. Be patient and make room for those traveling lighter or more quickly than you, and keep noise to a minimum.

It should go without saying, but remember that pets are not permitted in the backcountry of either park.

Respect park regulations. They have been created to help give you a safe, wilderness experience. Stick to the itinerary that you have scheduled, always staying in the campsites that you have reserved.

One last thing. Try leaving your bright gas lantern at home. When your eyes adjust to the darkness you will find that a few well-placed candle lanterns are really all the light you need.

While some of these suggestions may seem nitpicky, they can actually be fun to implement. They are practical and symbolic examples of how we must adapt to a changing reality. When practiced, you can be assured that the impact of your presence is being minimized and that's the way it should be.

5. The Outfit

There is a wide range of gear you'll want to consider in order to make your paddling experience safe and enjoyable. If you are already an outdoor enthusiast, you may have much of the gear you'll need for paddling the waters of the Yellowstone-Teton area safely and in comfort.

Be sure to carefully read Chapter 1, Safety on the Water and in the Wilderness, to get a clear understanding of the paddling risks and how to assess them and to give you a better idea of what equipment is required for the varied conditions of paddling on a mountain lake.

If you are new to the paddling sports or are considering a backcountry paddling experience for the first time, this overview of equipment should help you get organized and feel confident that you are well prepared. It also explains what is recommended for paddling the waters of the Yellowstone-Teton area.

If you are going out for a day trip, there are certain items that are a must. Consult the day trip equipment list (see page 38) so that you don't forget key items that would compromise your safety and comfort. On longer trips that involve overnight stays in remote places, the list of equipment grows in length to include all the items necessary to help you become self-sufficient and equipped for a range of conditions and experiences.

CANOES AND KAYAKS

Paddling the lakes of Yellowstone and Teton parks can take place with two types of water craft: canoes and sea kayaks. Canoes have been, and still are, the craft of choice for paddling these waters, but sea kayaks are gaining in popularity as people come to understand their special qualities. Both are small, responsive craft that provide the means to travel across open water simply and self-sufficiently. Both offer low-impact, upper body, aerobic exercise that can be as leisurely or as strenuous as you want to make it. Both are for people who want to enjoy an exhilarating, yet contemplative, activity. Both allow you to explore the world of lakes and rivers in very much the same way people have for thousands of years.

Canoes, compared to sea kayaks, are wider, deeper, open boats, which are generally paddled by two people, each using a single-bladed paddle. With a basic hull design that has changed very little from the earliest Native American boats, they can carry hundreds of pounds of cargo.

On the other hand, sea kayaks, or touring kayaks, are narrower, have a closed deck and sealed cockpit to shed water, use a double-bladed paddle, and are generally paddled solo. They have a lower center of gravity than canoes, making them much more stable than commonly believed. Their lower profile also reduces their susceptibility to the effects of waves and wind.

The author, keeping a low profile in his kayak on the South Arm of Yellowstone Lake.

Like canoes, kayaks are capable of carrying large loads. While gear is not as conveniently accessible in a kayak, it is more protected from water by the enclosed hull.

There are numerous styles and models of both craft available through outdoor equipment stores and by mail order. Explore the pros and cons before renting or purchasing, and consider using both craft if you are traveling as a group. In that way you can compare their differences in the field.

EQUIPMENT

The equipment and gear you take along depends to a large extent on the type and length of trip you are planning. The choices you make will also vary depending on whether you are going solo, or with a partner, a group, or your family. Will you have to plan your gear so you can be totally self-reliant, or can you share group gear with others?

Paddling the lakes of the Yellowstone-Teton area requires almost no portaging, so you can pack heavier than if you were backpacking, but don't go overboard. An overloaded boat in rough water can capsize more easily than a wisely loaded boat. At the same time, the traveler who packs too lightly without the proper gear can be at severe risk. Look over the equipment lists on pages 38 and 39 and plan for all situations. Ultimately, your own experiences and preferences will dictate your choice of equipment.

CLOTHING

The human body, for all practical purposes, is hairless. This unprotected nakedness renders it poorly suited to living with comfort in the outdoors of the Rocky Mountain West. The body heats itself by metabolizing food that has been consumed, and it loses heat in five ways: conduction, convection, radiation, respiration, and evaporation. Paying attention to both fueling the body and to heat loss is key to maintaining your comfort while paddling on the cold waters and in the high altitudes of the area.

Conduction takes place when the body comes in contact with a solid object that is cooler than the body, such as a rock or cold, sandy beach. This encourages heat to move away from the body into the object. Convection occurs when body heat is transferred away from it by coming in contact with moving fluids, such as air or water. This is the classic heat loss when you are paddling. Radiation, on the other hand, takes place anytime the heat from a warm body is transferred, or radiated, into the space around it. Putting on a warm hat and layers that insulate the body helps slow down this kind of heat loss. When a human breathes, heat from the body, along with moisture, is exhaled from the nose and mouth, and cooler air is inhaled and heated by the body. During the respiration process, then, some body heat is lost. Lastly, heat is taken away from the body through the evaporation of perspiration off of the body's surface. This is one of the most effective means the body has for dumping excess heat when it is too warm, but it can also result in damp clothing and unwanted heat loss during times of exercise in cold, windy conditions.

All five aspects of heat loss are taking place simultaneously and to varying degrees 24 hours a day. To live comfortably in the outdoors you must be aware of heat loss and prevent it when it is unwanted.

Keep in mind another important consideration. The human body is made up of a large warm core with extremities that have a large surface area compared to their volume. This is especially true of the final extremities, the fingers and toes. When the body core, made up of muscles and organs, is overheating, it tries to dump excess heat out through the extremities and through the head, where up to half of body heat is lost. In cold and wet conditions, unwanted heat loss may take place through the extremities. To conserve body heat in these conditions, protect the head and extremities from heat loss. Simply wearing a hat or slipping on a pair of gloves can help reduce heat loss tremendously.

Having the proper clothing can make the difference between success and failure, comfort and pain, in the wilderness. By using three basic layers—one for wicking moisture away from the body, a second for insulation, and a third for wind and rain protection—you'll be well on your way to living comfortably. Most outdoor recreationists today use synthetics and wool for inner layers, with a waterproof but breathable outer layer to protect from wind, rain, spray, or snow. Loose fitting layers allow you to stay comfortable and dry as outside conditions change and as your body's temperature and moisture output vary.

A word to the wise: If you wear cotton in the outdoors, especially next to your skin, it will not dry after becoming wet. It will keep you cold and wet and can easily contribute to hypothermia. Leave it at home.

FOOD AND COOKING

There is hardly any subject related to living outdoors that has such a range of opinions and philosophies as the subject of food and its preparation. There are vegetarians and meat eaters. There are gourmets preparing extravagant meals from fresh foods. There are "minimalists" who thrive on simplicity, whether they are using fresh or dried foods.

Numerous books and magazine articles present the range of possibilities for outdoor dining, but for the purposes of this book, suffice it to say that there are just three things to consider as you plan this portion of your trip: the length of the trip, how many people are going along, and the purpose of the trip. Trip length and the number of people, and their food preferences, are somewhat obvious elements of your planning. The purpose of the trip, however, may not be as obvious. It is a key element, though, because it relates to the length and pace of the trip and therefore the choice of foods and their preparation. For example, will you be going out for a leisurely few hours of paddling, or will you be paddling long days and eating "on the run," arriving at camp late? Will you be spending a lot of leisure time in and around camp?

There are many good recipes and menus available to guide your planning. The goal, however, is quite simple: You are trying to replenish the energy and nutrients expended getting you to where you are going, and you are trying to do that in a way that is appetizing and, I would add, relatively simple to prepare.

Men burn about 2,700 calories per day and women about 2,000. A paddler burns about 150 to 400 calories per hour depending on how strenuous the conditions are. Carbohydrates, proteins, and fats are the energy sources you are looking for to replenish those burned calories.

Carbohydrates can be found in grains, grain-based foods such as breads and cereals, and in fruits and vegetables. These are important, especially on extended trips, so make them at least half of your diet. Candy, a refined sugar carbohydrate, while not supplying nutrients, is a good source of energy, and having some on hand to supplement your diet can be a good idea.

Proteins are extremely important in maintaining healthy cells and supplying many other physiological needs. Whole proteins (meat, fish, chicken, eggs, and cheese) can be consumed in smaller amounts; recommendations usually call for a little more than a quarter-pound per day. When possible, try getting proteins from plant foods such as rice, beans, and peas (you'll have to consume more than a quarter-pound per day), rather than from highly saturated fat foods like red meat. Speaking of fats, they are an important nutrient, but only small amounts (a few teaspoons) each day will fulfill body requirements.

Water consumption is discussed in greater detail in the section, "Dehydration," page 11, but always remember that it is a nutrient that improves the digestion and absorption of the foods discussed above, and it is an important help in maintaining energy levels. Be sure to bring a good water filter along. Even though the water in the area is amazingly pristine and looks pure, it can contain substances that may make you ill. To be on the safe side, always filter water. If you do not have a filter along for your trip, the water should be heated to boiling.

Food choices can range from fresh foods to prepackaged, freeze-dried selections to home dehydrated assortments, or a mix of all of these. Since trips into the lake areas of Yellowstone and the Tetons will by nature be only a few days in length, nutrition is less important than energy replenishment and appeal. Mix up the menu some and, for the fun of it, include some treats. Have hot food and hot drinks for cold or wet times and easy-to-prepare meals for simplicity's sake or for those times when you've reached camp after dark or you're just plain weary.

Plan at least one special meal to look forward to. And don't forget a spice kit. It is the key to creating a varied menu.

There are many pots and pan sets available on the market, or if you are new to this and do not want to invest the money, you may try to piece together a set from your home kitchen. Whatever you choose, make sure the cooking gear is compact and nests well.

Heating water and cooking food is done most efficiently on a portable camping or backpacking stove as opposed to using a campfire. While stoves lack the ambiance that many associate with a backcountry experience, they are clean, quick, and better for the environment. Remember that fires are prohibited at many of the backcountry paddling sites in the Tetons and Yellowstone. Always be prepared for cooking with a stove, and if fires are important to you, make sure the site you choose allows them.

PACKING

You can be assured that in any paddling situation equipment will come in contact with water. Let's face it. Rain, spray, and submersion happen. Yet it is amazing how many travelers do not pack their gear with this reality in mind. Be prepared for the inevitable!

There are a multitude of waterproof dry bags and boxes available in all sizes that will keep gear protected in the harshest conditions. Heavy-duty plastic bags are a less expensive alternative and work well if they are used with care to prevent tears and punctures. Zipper-locked bags are great for all your small personal items and for packaging food. Doublebag any item which would be rendered useless if it becomes wet. Not only is a wet sleeping bag a nuisance, but it can greatly increase the risks to your safety.

If you are traveling by canoe, pack equipment into as few packs as possible to facilitate packing and transportation and to minimize loose and small items that

The kayaker's gear must be packed in small bags that fit through the deck hatches.

may become lost in an upset. Gear should be secured when you are on the water, but some experienced paddlers feel that tying in very heavy packs may contribute to a canoe sinking in a capsize. This can be true, but gear packed in waterproof dry bags can also hold enough air to actually float a boat. Use your best judgment.

The person traveling by kayak will pack differently than the canoeist, using smaller packages so that gear can be stuffed into every available nook and cranny. Even though gear is more protected in the covered deck of a kayak, be sure to use waterproof containers.

Whether you are traveling by canoe or kayak, it is helpful to color code or label containers. You'll find items more easily.

EQUIPMENT CHECKLIST

The following checklist of equipment contains suggestions for both essential and optional items. (The *c* or *k* after some items denotes that item is for use with a *c*anoe or a *k*ayak.)

Boat and Accessories

- ❑ canoe
- ❑ kayak
- ❑ paddles (with at least one spare)
- ❑ life jacket (personal flotation device, or PFD)
- ❑ ropes for bow line and for securing gear
- ❑ spray skirt (k)
- ❑ waterproof storage bags
- ❑ paddle float for self-rescue (k)
- ❑ sponge
- ❑ bailer or bilge pump
- ❑ flotation bags (k) (optional)
- ❑ paddle leash (k) (optional)
- ❑ deck bag (k) (optional)

Emergency and navigational equipment

- ❑ map/charts and map case (or a zipper-locked bag to keep maps dry)
- ❑ compass
- ❑ binoculars
- ❑ knife
- ❑ whistle
- ❑ waterproof matches, lighter, fire starter
- ❑ repair kit
- ❑ multipurpose tool (Leatherman-type)
- ❑ duct tape
- ❑ high-energy food bars and drink
- ❑ light rope, parachute cord

First-aid kit

- ❑ first-aid book
- ❑ adhesive bandages
- ❑ butterfly closures
- ❑ sterile compresses
- ❑ gauze roll

- ❑ adhesive tape
- ❑ Ace bandage
- ❑ triangular bandage
- ❑ first-aid and burn ointment
- ❑ skin lotion
- ❑ petroleum jelly
- ❑ safety pins
- ❑ aspirin and pain pills
- ❑ tweezers
- ❑ needle
- ❑ moleskin and blister kit

Clothing

- ❑ shorts (fast drying)
- ❑ long pants (fast drying)
- ❑ short-sleeved polypropylene shirt
- ❑ long-sleeved polypropylene shirt
- ❑ light pile jacket or wool shirt
- ❑ wind parka
- ❑ rain parka and pants
- ❑ baseball cap
- ❑ broad-brimmed hat
- ❑ waterproof sandals and/or aqua socks
- ❑ cotton bandanna

Miscellaneous

- ❑ sunglasses with strap
- ❑ water bottles
- ❑ water filter
- ❑ sun block
- ❑ lip balm/block
- ❑ insect repellent
- ❑ fishing permit
- ❑ boat permit
- ❑ food and beverages
- ❑ trash bag

The following additional equipment is recommended for multi-day trips:

Emergency and navigational equipment

- ❏ flares, signaling device, strobe
- ❏ emergency shelter, tarp, space blanket

Repair kit

- ❏ boat spare parts, as necessary
- ❏ mattress repair kit, as necessary
- ❏ light wire
- ❏ stove repair kit
- ❏ sewing kit
- ❏ glasses repair kit
- ❏ seam sealer

Camping gear

- ❏ tent and fly
- ❏ ground sheet
- ❏ rain fly for dining
- ❏ sleeping bag (in a waterproof bag)
- ❏ pad/mattress
- ❏ toilet kit
- ❏ toilet paper
- ❏ trowel
- ❏ flashlight and/or head lamp
- ❏ towel
- ❏ canoe packs, kayak dry bags, duffel bags, or large mesh bags
- ❏ candle lantern
- ❏ bear pole ropes, block and tackle for hanging food
- ❏ small inflatable or folding camp chair (optional)

Clothing

- ❏ underwear
- ❏ socks
- ❏ polypropylene/pile gloves
- ❏ camp shoes
- ❏ paddling gloves or pogies (k)
- ❏ sleepwear
- ❏ mosquito net hat
- ❏ wet suit/dry suit (optional)

Cooking equipment

- ❏ stove and fuel
- ❏ cook kit and frying pan
- ❏ eating and cooking utensils
- ❏ cup and/or bowl and/or plate
- ❏ water bottles, jugs
- ❏ potholder
- ❏ charcoal grill (optional)
- ❏ dutch oven (optional)
- ❏ food storage bags
- ❏ dish soap and scrubber
- ❏ matches, lighter
- ❏ spices and condiments

Miscellaneous

- ❏ Backcountry Use Permit
- ❏ notebook, pen/pencil
- ❏ camera and film (optional)
- ❏ musical instruments (optional)
- ❏ reading materials (optional)
- ❏ camelback water container (optional)

6. Paddling Trips in Yellowstone National Park

While nonmotorized, hand-propelled boats are permitted on most lakes in Yellowstone National Park, Yellowstone, Lewis, and Shoshone lakes are the largest and most easily accessible.

Yellowstone Lake is a vast expanse of water, encompassing 136 square miles, with 20-mile stretches of open water and 110 miles of shoreline, 80 of which are accessible only by boat or on foot.

Lewis Lake, just a short drive down the main park road from Yellowstone Lake, has a boat launch and a large campground on the southeast edge of the lake. Motorized boats are allowed on this lake, but conflicts with hand-propelled craft are negligible. This is the body of water you must cross to access the backcountry of the much larger Shoshone Lake. Lewis Lake is a beautiful lake in its own right, though. There are beaches, a small hot spring thermal area, water birds and pelicans to watch, good fishing, and great views of the Red Mountains and Mount Sheridan.

Shoshone Lake, the largest backcountry lake in the lower 48 states and Yellowstone's second largest lake, is reached by paddling and wading upstream 3.5 miles on the Lewis River Channel that flows into the north end of Lewis Lake. This river segment is the only river in Yellowstone on which you may operate a boat, and it must be self-propelled.

Yellowstone National Park

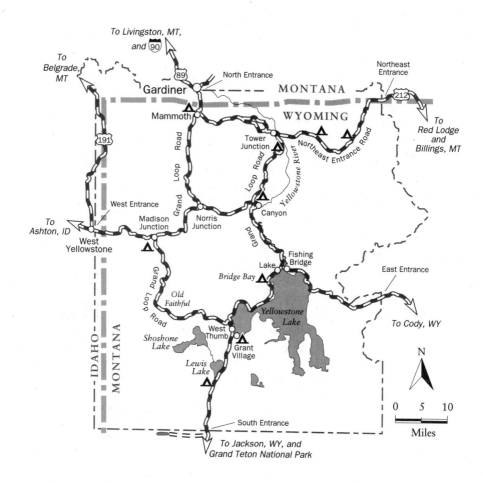

Day trips

There are many possible day trips on the park's three biggest lakes. Lewis Lake has two launch points; however, the preferable access is the boat launch at the south end of the lake. This launch point is situated to better avoid wind and wave conditions found on the north shore. Pay attention to current and foreseeable weather conditions, and consider whether or not increased wave action may make returning to your launch spot a dangerous route. Consult the ranger station near the campground at Lewis Lake if you have any questions or concerns about paddling.

Access to paddling on Yellowstone Lake is most convenient at launch sites located at Grant Village, Bridge Bay Marina, and Sedge Bay. If you have questions about access or route selection, visit or call the ranger station at Lake or Bridge Bay.

1 Lewis Lake

Character: This trip explores the shoreline of Lewis Lake, named by trappers in honor of Captain Meriwether Lewis of the Lewis and Clark Expedition. It is a good choice for those seeking a full or part day, straightforward shoreline paddle with time to fish, bird watch, or explore on and off the shore.

See map on page 43

Total paddling distance: 9 miles if the entire shoreline is paddled.
Average paddling time: 4–8 hours.
Put-in and take-out: Lewis Lake boat launch.
Difficulty: Moderate.
Be aware of: Afternoon winds and accompanying waves, thin crust and hot water at the thermal basin, possible motorboats.
Attractions: Scenery and hot spring at the Lewis Lake outlet, sandy beaches, a small thermal basin, the Lewis River Channel inlet and river paddle, views of the Red Mountains, fishing, wildlife viewing.
Maps: USGS 7.5-minute Mt. Sheridan–WY, Lewis Falls–WY.
Use: Light to moderate.
Directions: The Lewis Lake boat launch is on the South Entrance Road 11.1 miles north of Yellowstone's South Entrance and 8.3 miles south of Grant Village Junction where the South Entrance Road is joined by the road to Grant Village.

The paddling: The trip starts and ends at the Lewis Lake boat launch, located at the far southern edge of the lake. The boat launch can be busy at times since it is used as the starting point for paddlers heading into the Shoshone Lake backcountry, and for day-use paddlers and motorboat operators, but once you launch you leave the crowds behind. There is an 85-unit campground, a picnic area, a ranger station, and pit toilets available at the put-in. After you have unloaded your equipment, make room for others by parking your vehicle at the larger parking area located to the east; it is behind the toilets and across from the ranger station.

Lewis Lake

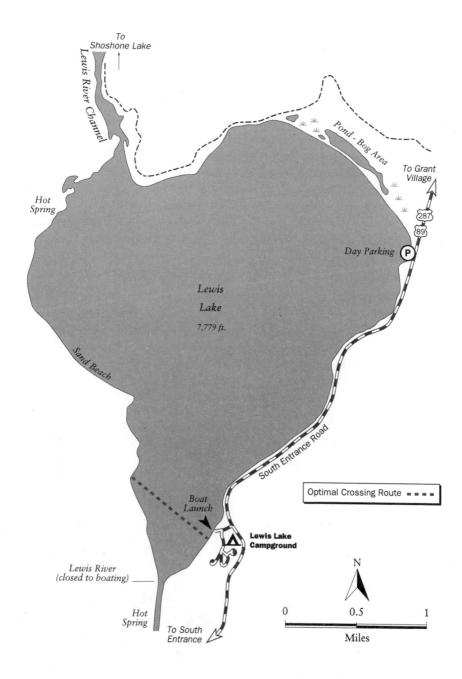

To
Shoshone Lake

Lewis River Channel

Pond - Bog Area

To Grant
Village

287
89

Hot
Spring

Day Parking **P**

Lewis
Lake

7,779 ft.

Sand Beach

South Entrance Road

Optimal Crossing Route ▪ ▪ ▪ ▪

Boat
Launch

Lewis Lake
Campground

N

Lewis River
(closed to boating)

Hot
Spring

To South
Entrance

0   0.5   1

Miles

This trip is a clockwise exploration of Lewis Lake. Any part of the 9-mile shoreline can be paddled, depending on time you have available and your inclination. If you choose not to paddle the entire shoreline, retrace your route, avoiding a lake crossing in the afternoon when high winds can make conditions risky, if not dangerous.

From the boat launch, head along the shoreline to the left. You'll notice evidence of the campground hidden in the trees and might see anglers trying their luck along the shore. In about 0.5 mile, you'll approach the outlet of the Lewis River Channel. While it is closed to paddling, the setting is beautiful as the lake's shoreline merges with the river. You may see steam rising from the tiny hot springs just downstream on the west bank. If the sky is clear, you'll see the peaks of the northernmost mountains of Grand Teton National Park to the south.

Look and listen for birds here and along the entire shoreline of the lake. Bring along binoculars and a field guide to assist in identifying what you see. Be alert for common mergansers, those low-riding ducks with the long thin bill adapted for catching fish. Look, too, for the rust-colored head of the female and the group of ducklings that so often are in her company. The male merganser has a dark green head. They can be seen weaving in and out of obstacles along the shoreline, but don't get so close that you alarm them or interfere with their food gathering.

The beaches at the north end of Lewis Lake provide good choices for a rest stop.

White pelicans summer in the Yellowstone area and can often be seen on the lake. While they can be confused with swans from a distance, they have an unmistakable profile, an average wingspan of 9 feet, and they fly in a flock. Swans will usually be seen solo or in pairs.

As you paddle northward along the west shore, watch for other life on shore and overhead. Moose and elk inhabit the area. Bald eagles and ospreys, their smaller "cousin" with the bent-back wings, may be passing overhead as they search the water for a meal of fish.

While the clean, clear water of this lake attracts many anglers today, this has not always been the case. Lewis Falls, just downstream from the lake, historically created a barrier to fish migration and kept the lake barren until 1890 when the U.S. Fish and Wildlife Service stocked the lake with lake trout from Lake Michigan and Loch Leven brown trout from Scotland. These fish have done so well in Lewis and Shoshone lakes that on occasion lake trout have been shipped back to Lake Michigan to help restock its fish population which was decimated by lamprey eels.

About a mile north of the river outlet are some sandy beaches perfect for a rest stop, snack, and a view of the Red Mountains to the east. This area is also a good place to take some time to fish from shore or to wander into the woods. Scan the meadows to the west and north for possible elk.

The shore swings more to the west as you head to a small thermal basin about 1.5 miles north of the beach. If you choose to take a closer look, use great care on shore. Thermal areas are fragile and easily damaged by careless walking, and the crust can be dangerously thin, possibly breaking and plunging you into very hot water. While these little springs are much smaller than the park's other vast thermal basins, they are indicative of the tremendous heat below the earth's surface and the continual cycling of water on this planet. This is a thermal feature you can explore with few, if any, visitors in your midst.

Within about 0.5 mile you'll come to where the Lewis River Channel enters the lake. If the water surface is calm, you may be able to see an underwater hot spring. Paddle around slowly about 100 feet from the west shore, out where the river enters the lake, looking closely for the flattened cone and the blue and green of the hot-water vent. Sometimes you can even feel a slight warming of the water temperature at the surface.

At this point you have a decision to make. If you have the time and the energy, a paddle partway up the river can be a nice change of pace. If you decide to paddle the river, consult trip 2 for details. You can choose to continue east along the north shore of Lewis Lake, but keep in mind that you have paddled a little less than half of the shoreline. It is also important to note that the north and east shore can experience 2- to 3-foot waves in the afternoon. Only experienced paddlers with proper safety equipment and practiced safety techniques should attempt this route; others should retrace the west shore route back to the boat launch.

If you are continuing east, you may see an occasional hiker walking the trail along the north end of the lake. Hikers in this area are usually going to the Lewis River Channel for the day. There are more nice beaches along this stretch and a pond and bog area just back in the woods on the northeast shore. This may be a good time to take a snack break, a rest, and a look around before you begin the last leg of the paddle southward to the boat launch.

Just as you begin your swing southward you may notice the park road as it comes near the lake and parallels the shore to the boat launch. The launch is 2.5 miles to the south, or at least 1 hour of paddling, depending on conditions. If the wind has picked up, there will be an increase in waves, too, so use caution and keep within a safe distance of shore. This entire shoreline receives the oncoming waves from across the lake; it is also steeper, and a landing here is more difficult than elsewhere around the lake.

2 Lewis River Channel

Character: This day trip proceeds along the north shore of Lewis Lake to the Lewis River Channel and

See map on page 43

includes a leisurely paddle up the river for approximately 2 miles. At this point, you are halted in your upstream paddle by the increase in water flow. Your relaxed float downstream to the lake is followed by the return across the north shore, for which caution is required.

Total paddling distance: Approximately 9 miles.

Average paddling time: 4–6 hours.

Put-in and take-out: Parking pullout on the northeast side of Lewis Lake.

Difficulty: Moderate.

Be aware of: Wind and waves on Lewis Lake, especially in the afternoon; some obstacles (rocks and trees) in the river channel.

Attractions: Fishing, bird watching (especially ospreys and eagles), small thermal area.

Maps: USGS 7.5-minute Mt. Sheridan–WY, Lewis Falls–WY.

Use: Moderate to heavy in the river channel.

Directions: The parking pullout on the northeast side of Lewis Lake is located on the west side of South Entrance Road, 2.5 miles north of the turnoff to the Lewis Lake boat launch and 5.8 miles south of Grant Village Junction, where the road to Grant Village joins the main road.

The paddling: This half-day trip takes you along the 2.5-mile north shore of Lewis Lake to where the Lewis River Channel enters the lake at the west side. Be aware that waves of 2 to 3 feet can typically build up in the afternoons along this route. Get an early start so that you can arrive back at the take-out before conditions become rough. Turning upstream, paddle the relatively smooth first 2 miles of the Lewis River Channel to where the current increases, making progress difficult. The exact turnaround point is up to you: It will depend on your physical strength and time available.

As you enter the lower stretch of the river you'll find a very different world than the lake, one more secluded and protected from the wind. In this area the river is wide, at least 100 yards, and the current is calm enough that beds of lily pads and "fields" of underwater grasses have taken hold on the sand and gravel river bottom. The water is very clear and cold, supporting a healthy trout population and therefore the wildlife that feeds on it. The aquatic ecosystems of Yellowstone are an important and integral component of the larger ecological systems of the park and beyond.

The tiniest headwater creeks, high up in the mountains, are the first to contribute to the aquatic ecosystems. As these creeks flow into and blend with the waters of progressively larger streams and rivers, simple plant and animal life becomes increasingly more complex. The smallest inhabitants become food for larger creatures, with fish eventually enjoying a place at the top of the aquatic food chain. However, since one life form depends on another to live, larger inhabitants of the terrestrial landscape, including otters, various birds, bears, and humans, will then prey upon the fish. The waters of Yellowstone are a fine example of the intricate complexity that exists within and between the various ecosystems that make up Yellowstone Park.

There are many fine books available to help you learn more about the fish that inhabit Yellowstone. A partial list includes *Fishing Yellowstone National Park* by Richard Parks (Falcon, 1998); *Freshwater Wilderness: Yellowstone Fishes and Their World* by John D. Varley and Paul Schullery (Yellowstone Library and Museum Association, 1983); and *Fishing Yellowstone Hatches* by John Juracek and Craig Mathews (Lyons and Burford, 1992).

Park surveys also reveal some interesting facts about Yellowstone's fish populations. The most commonly caught fish is the cutthroat, followed in order by rainbow, brown, brook, and lake trout. Grayling, that fish with the very large dorsal fin, and whitefish are caught in smaller numbers. The average size of fish caught in the park is about 14 inches, and trout as big as 3 pounds are common.

Watch closely for fish as you paddle along, particularly cutthroat, the trout with the red throat slash, and brown trout, with their red- and orange-spotted sides. Introduced into the park in the 1890s, browns spawn in the fall. Streams like the Lewis River Channel are popular fishing spots in October. The channel is also a good place to fish for brook trout, identified by red, yellow, and pink dots on their sides.

About 90 percent of the fish caught in Yellowstone are released. The practice of catch-and-release is required in most waters of Yellowstone, but it is encouraged in all the waters. Releasing fish leaves them available for other members of the food chain and for future generations of visiting humans.

Be conscious also of anglers who have hiked in on the trail that parallels the east bank of the river. Try your best to share the river with them by not paddling too close to where they are fishing.

A kayaker paddles beneath the rock outcrop on the Lewis River Channel.

You may see other paddlers on the river, some of whom are returning from the Shoshone Lake backcountry. Paddlers moving downstream have the right of way and may be moving quickly in the narrower sections. Give them room to maneuver around obstacles, and assume that they, just as you, are seeking solitude. Respect that by keeping disturbances to a minimum.

As you paddle the river, steer clear of the occasional trees that have fallen into the water. While this area was only partially burned by the 1988 fires, the number of trees in the water has increased and can create a hazard. These trees provide protective habitat for fish and are also a good place to look for waterfowl as they too "paddle" along the banks. On the shore, the standing dead trees, or snags, also provide habitat and nesting opportunities for woodpeckers that have moved in to feed on insects working on the dead trees. Hairy woodpeckers and the similar, but smaller, downy are common, and their hollow tapping on trees can often be heard. So, too, can the loud rattling call of the belted kingfisher. Look for this distinctive, big-headed blue-and-white bird with the large bill and tall crest. A small bird, but larger than a robin, it will be seen alone or in pairs sitting patiently on a tree limb or darting from place to place as it searches for fish to eat.

Approximately one-third of the way up the river, about 1 mile from Lewis Lake, the river takes a brief, abrupt turn to the left before continuing northward.

At this point there is a large rock outcrop on the right, perched about 20 feet above the water. Pull in to the right of the rock and beach your craft. You can scramble up the short trail for a good perspective of the river. This is a great place to take a break, enjoy the view, or eat lunch.

After this turn in the river, and as it begins to move north again, sandy beaches and islands become more common. Look for shorebirds scurrying along the sand and waterfowl, such as the low-riding mergansers and common goldeneye. The male goldeneye has a dark green, almost black, head with a round, white patch in front of the eye. A short distance past the northward turn in the river, look on the right bank for steam rising from a small hot spring and hot water that flows into the river.

The current will begin to pick up speed after the northward turn in the river, and your paddling effort, especially around sand bars and small islands, will also have to increase. You may want to turn back downstream in this area, but with some effort you can proceed farther upstream another 10 to 15 minutes, moving through faster, but shallow water.

Wherever you decide to turn back, relax and enjoy being carried back downstream by the flow of the current you worked against. Until the river widens again and the current slows, only an occasional stroke of the paddle is necessary to keep you on course. Since you now are paddling with the current, you will soon be back at Lewis Lake.

A word to the wise: At any time, but especially after noon, expect wind, and perhaps strong wind, as you enter the lake. Assess conditions carefully and use caution as you head left along the shore to the parking area, staying close to shore if waves have picked up. Within 30 to 45 minutes you can be back to your vehicle. If the wind makes it difficult to paddle or waves threaten to swamp your boat, go immediately to shore and wait until lake conditions calm before continuing, rather than put yourself at risk.

YELLOWSTONE LAKE

3 Grant Village to West Thumb Geyser Basin

Character: This half-day trip takes you north from Grant Village, past the West Thumb Geyser Basin and Potts Hot Spring Basin, providing a unique lake-view perspective of these two thermal areas, before returning to the put-in.

See map on pages 50–51

Total paddling distance: 5 miles.
Average paddling time: 2–3 hours.
Put-in and take-out: Grant Village boat launch.
Difficulty: Easy to moderate.
Be aware of: Afternoon wind and waves on the lake, no access to shore from the lake at the thermal basins.

Yellowstone Lake

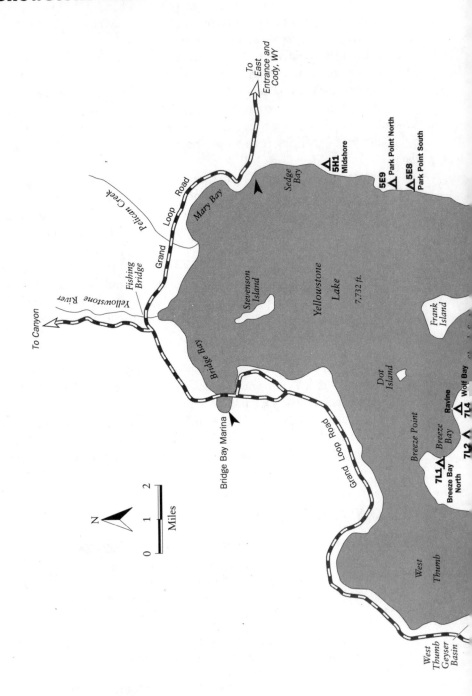

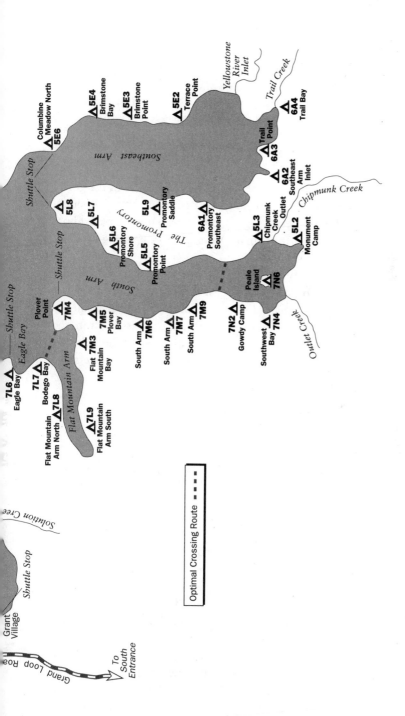

Optimal Crossing Route ▪ ▪ ▪ ▪

Attractions: Hot springs and geysers of the Lower Group, the Lake Shore Group 1500 feet to the north, and the Potts Hot Spring Basin 0.75 mile farther north.

Map: USGS 7.5-minute West Thumb–WY.

Use: Light.

Directions: The Grant Village boat launch is located by turning east at Grant Village Junction, 2.5 miles south of West Thumb, 8.3 miles north of Lewis Lake Campground, and 19.4 miles north of the South Entrance. After the turn to Grant Village, drive 1 mile to the first intersection and turn right at the Hamilton Store. Follow the signs down to the marina. It is most convenient to park at the right (south) end of the parking area.

The paddling: Once you reach the boat launch area, you can put in at the gravel beach to the left (north) end of the pier that parallels the parking area and lakeshore, immediately behind the park interpretive sign. You may also use the paved boat launch and paddle the short distance through the lagoon before entering the main lake a few hundred yards to the north.

This is a straightforward half-day paddle that takes you north along the west shore of the West Thumb of Yellowstone Lake, past three hot spring and geyser areas where you can view thermal activity from your craft. The Lower Group of the West Thumb Geyser Basin, the area you approach first, is accessible from the parking area at West Thumb. There is a system of boardwalks where visitors "from land" will be walking. From your boat you can see many of the same features they are viewing, including Fishing Cone, a partially submerged hot spring, and Lakeshore Geyser, a geyser which erupts up to 25 feet when active. On calm days, look for the submerged sinter shields (flattened domes) and cones of offshore hot springs.

Paddling another 1,500 feet or so to the north, you will soon come across the Lake Shore Group of the West Thumb Geyser Basin, located on a small strip of land between the lakeshore and the park highway. This area holds the basin's most active geysers, and since no direct land access is permitted, the view from your paddling location is as close as you can get. There are four geysers at this location, three of which erupt with relative frequency.

Occasional Geyser is quite active, erupting as frequently as every 30 minutes, with heights up to 10 feet. Its eruptions last 4 to 5 minutes. Like many other geysers, Occasional erupts from a vent at the top of a high platform of dissolved mineral deposits laid down over centuries of eruptions. This platform is so near Yellowstone Lake that runoff flows only several feet before plunging down a small falls into the lake.

Lone Pine, the largest geyser in the area, erupts less frequently, with intervals of 26 to 32 hours. Its waters jet up to 75 feet high and it's worth seeing, especially from your boat. Its first recorded activity was in 1974, and the geyser was named for the small pine tree located on the peninsula where the geyser vent is also located. Most geysers in the park change over time in eruption frequency and duration, and so it is with Lone Pine Geyser. In its early days, eruptions were more frequent than today's, but they were weaker and of shorter duration. Eruptions have now become quite predictable. Contact the ranger station to get an idea of when the next eruption is expected.

Overhanging Geyser is just that—a cone perched at the lake's edge. During eruptions, runoff falls directly to the lake's surface. While not a large geyser, erupting only 3 to 6 feet, it does erupt more frequently with intervals ranging from two to several hours and with flows lasting a few minutes to almost half an hour.

If you want to paddle about 20 minutes longer, you will come to Potts Hot Spring Basin, named for the trapper who visited and described the basin in 1826. It is an area rarely visited by the public. While it does contain geysers, they erupt erratically; the hot springs, however, are numerous. You'll see large amounts of steam rising from the basin, especially in the morning and on cooler days. By the way, fishing is prohibited in parts of this area. Check current regulations at a ranger station.

▮4▮ Grant Village to Breeze Point

Character: This trip follows the wooded shores and bluffs of the south and east shores of the West Thumb of Yellowstone Lake, exploring the long, sandy beaches at Breeze Point before retracing the route.

See map on pages 50–51

Total paddling distance: 12 miles.
Average paddling time: 6–8 hours.
Put-in and take-out: Grant Village boat launch.
Difficulty: Moderate.
Be aware of: Wind and waves, especially upon return.
Attractions: Large beach and spit area to roam and explore, full views of Yellowstone Lake with the Absaroka Range as a backdrop; ospreys, eagles, and other wildlife.
Maps: Trails Illustrated Yellowstone Lake Trail Map; USGS 7.5-minute West Thumb–WY, Mt. Sheridan–WY, Dot Island–WY.
Use: Light.
Directions: The Grant Village boat launch is located by turning east at Grant Village Junction, 2.5 miles south of West Thumb, 8.3 miles north of Lewis Lake Campground, and 19.4 miles north of the South Entrance. After the turn to Grant Village, drive 1 mile to the first intersection and turn right at the Hamilton Store. Follow the signs down to the marina. It is most convenient to park at the right (south) end of the parking area.

The paddling: This longer day trip offers a paddle on open water with a pleasant beach destination before returning to the boat launch at Grant Village. The route follows the wooded south shoreline and the bluffs on the east side of the West

Thumb. Look in the woods and along the shore for the occasional elk. When you begin to paddle due north, look for Solution Creek entering the lake. You can take a short diversion up this creek, knowing you have paddled 3.5 miles of the shoreline and are more than halfway to the destination, Breeze Point. Paddling very slowly and quietly, you may see young waterfowl accompanied by an adult as they learn to search for food on their own. Use great care and retreat to the main lake before disturbing them.

As you paddle north, look at the bluffs that expose flows of rhyolitic volcanic rock, rich, like granite, in silica. You get some good cross-sectional views of Yellowstone's long geologic history, including more "recent" volcanic flows caught in midmovement as they cooled. As you come around the shoreline to the east, roughly at the point where the "thumb" narrows down before entering the main part of Yellowstone Lake, there are several gravel beaches that can be a good place to rest, looking back over what you have just paddled and to the steam rising from the thermal basins. Paddling on again, in about 1.5 miles, you reach the unmistakable larger, sandy beaches just to the west of Breeze Point. This general area is the destination of this trip, so take all the time you want to explore the beaches and nearby woods, leaving enough time and energy for the 6-mile return trip. Rest in the sun and enjoy a lunch. Look on the sand for the large, horselike tracks of moose that have come down to the water to drink. Look, too, for the more delicate tracks of water and shore birds that frequent the area; you may just see evidence of pelicans. As everywhere along these shores, keep a sharp eye for bear tracks. They are rare but not unheard of along these beaches and are a reminder that you are in the wild midst of both the park and the Greater Yellowstone ecosystem.

A word to the wise: The name, Breeze Point, came about for obvious reasons: Waves can become large, commonly 2 to 3 feet by midday. Keep this in mind as you prepare to head back to the launch. The usual afternoon prevailing winds come from the southwest, which means you may be heading directly into them and their waves as you return across the West Thumb. Pace yourself and stay as close to shore as conditions dictate to assure your safety.

5 Bridge Bay to Pelican Creek

Character: Starting from the boating center of Yellowstone Lake, this trip follows the northwest shore, paddling past the historic Lake Hotel and on past the Yellowstone River as it flows from the lake, and then turning around at the mouth of Pelican Creek and returning.

See map on pages 50–51

Total paddling distance: 9 miles.
Average paddling time: 5–7 hours.
Put-in and take-out: Bridge Bay Marina boat launch.
Difficulty: Moderate.

Be aware of: Wind and waves.
Attractions: Views of historic Lake Hotel, outlet of Yellowstone River, Fishing Bridge Visitor Center, Pelican Creek inlet, migratory birds.
Maps: USGS 7.5-minute Lake Junction–WY and Lake Butte–WY.
Use: Light, once outside of Bridge Bay Marina.
Directions: Bridge Bay Marina is located 4 miles southwest of Lake Junction, immediately west of Fishing Bridge and 16 miles northeast of West Thumb. Once you turn into the Bridge Bay area, follow the signs to the boat launch. You can park temporarily at the launch or near the dock just to the right. When done unloading, move your vehicle to the parking lot immediately adjacent to the launch.

The paddling: This day paddle is along a section of Yellowstone Lake's shoreline that is less remote than other described day trips, but it is interesting because the route gives you different lake views and allows you to explore cultural and natural areas that are important to understanding Yellowstone Park.

Once you gear up and paddle out of Bridge Bay Marina, head to the left along the west shore. You'll notice vehicles moving along the park road that parallels the shore close by here. On your right, to the south, is Stevenson Island. Enjoy the views of the Absaroka Range, the rugged mountain backdrop to the east. In about 2.5 miles, you come to "the Lake area." The imposing Lake Hotel soon comes into sight. You cannot miss the 300-foot-wide, four-story structure with 50-foot-high Ionic columns. For more than 100 years visitors have been coming to this landmark to dine and rest.

Early tourists who ventured deep enough into the park to reach Yellowstone Lake lodged at a small tent camp. A more permanent lodging was constructed to replace this camp, but by 1891 only one wing of 80 rooms had been completed. In 1903 and 1904, further construction increased the number of rooms to 210, large enough to house well over 400 guests. Other than the absence of the string of horse-drawn "Yellowstone Wagons" of yesteryear, today's visitor will view the light yellow-and-white building very much as it appeared early in the century. Fine meals and string quartets playing classical music still greet the visitor of the twentieth and twenty-first centuries who travels to this serene setting. While finding a suitable beach to land your boat is not easy, and climbing the bank to the hotel can be steep, you still may want to go ashore to see the hotel more closely or have lunch in the dining room.

At this point you are about 1 mile from where the Yellowstone River leaves Yellowstone Lake. As you paddle to the outlet, you should notice signs prohibiting travel by boat down the river. Even with this restriction, you can begin to get a feel for the new power the river is now taking on. After beginning its journey in the Absaroka Mountains to the south, the relatively small river flows into the southern end of Yellowstone Lake's Southeast Arm and begins its long journey northward, eventually joining the Missouri River in the northeast corner of Montana. A short way downstream from the outlet the river flows over the LeHardy Rapids, through the vast Hayden Valley, plunges over the Upper and Lower falls of the Yellowstone, and then carves its way through the Grand Canyon of the Yellowstone. All this can be visited by vehicle, but it begins here, where the lake drains its contents.

As you travel to the east you are paddling the northernmost shoreline of Yellowstone Lake, and within a short distance you reach the beaches of the Fishing Bridge area. Your first indication that you are near the historic Fishing Bridge Visitor Center, nestled back in the woods, may be the sight of people enjoying themselves on the beach. Pull onto shore anywhere in this area and wander up to the visitor center and museum. The building is a beautiful lodgepole pine structure, the first one of its kind constructed within a national park. Take a close look at the details of the shingle-and-log construction before going in.

Once inside you see stuffed examples of birds and mammals common to the area. These will help you to better identify and understand the many creatures that inhabit this varied landscape through the summer months. The Yellowstone Association for Natural Science, History and Education also operates a very good bookstore at this location.

If you have time for a longer stay, stop by the National Park Service counter in the visitor center to check their schedule of guided walks in the area. There is no better way to learn about this naturally beautiful and historic area of the park.

There are restrooms here, and across the street is a Hamilton Store gift shop, grocery, and ice cream stand.

The last leg of this 9-mile paddle is the remaining 1 mile to the inlet of Pelican Creek. This creek is born to the north, high in the mountains of the Mirror Plateau, and it meanders through the Pelican Valley before reaching Yellowstone Lake. You may not paddle into the creek, but think for a moment about the landscape this stream drains as it flows through the wilderness habitat of elk, grizzly bears, and wolves. It is another reminder of Yellowstone's wildness.

Throughout this entire stretch keep your eyes alert for pelicans. They are commonly seen flying overhead or almost skimming the water's surface, and large flocks can often be found resting at the inlet of the creek. Also look for ospreys and bald eagles perched in trees near the shoreline or gliding over the lake looking for fish. This is the turnaround point to begin heading back to Bridge Bay.

A word to the wise: Waves, building up as they cross the lake, can become relatively high in this area, so stay close to shore in case you need to make an emergency landing.

6 Sedge Bay

Character: An open-ended trip that gives you a taste of paddling the east shore of Yellowstone Lake and shows how easily you can leave civilization behind in Yellowstone.

See map on pages 50–51

Total paddling distance: Optional.
Average paddling time: No specific time.
Put-in and take-out: Sedge Bay boat launch.
Difficulty: Moderate.
Be aware of: Wind and waves, especially in the afternoon.
Attractions: Waterfowl and birdlife; interesting and jagged shoreline.
Maps: USGS 7.5-minute Lake Butte–WY and Frank Island–WY.
Use: Light.
Directions: Sedge Bay is located at the northeast corner of Yellowstone Lake, just southeast of the more prominent Mary Bay. The Sedge Bay boat launch can be reached by driving approximately 8 miles east from Fishing Bridge to the last parking area before the road goes uphill and inland from the shoreline. Look for a pullout on the right between the road and the shore.

The paddling: You will find a large beach area at Sedge Bay and perhaps other paddlers preparing to head out. Most paddlers embarking from here are heading into the backcountry for an overnight experience, but this also is a great place to start a day trip, the length of which can be completely up to you.

Canoeists, kayakers, and motorboat operators preparing to launch share the beach on Sedge Bay.

Be sure to leave early in the day. The east shore of the lake is particularly susceptible to large waves in the afternoon as prevailing winds have gathered strength across the entire width of the lake. Use caution and return early to avoid rough conditions. Plan to include time for slower return paddling.

Once you leave the boat launch, simply head south down the shoreline, exploring as you go. There are some interesting rock outcrops along the way, and keep alert to birds flying overhead or roosting in trees at the shoreline. You are most likely to see ospreys, pelicans, and perhaps bald eagles fishing the lake waters. These are both good examples of the larger, fish-eating birds that migrate to Yellowstone to nest for the summer. Because of its 5- to 6-foot wingspan and black-and-white markings, the osprey from a distance is often mistaken for a bald eagle, but look for the obviously crooked wings that distinguish it. If you are lucky enough to see it fishing, notice that it hovers on beating wings and dives feet first, our only hawk that dives into the water. Its call is a series of sharp *"cheep, cheep"* whistles, or when annoyed or near its nest, more of a *"cheererk!"* Its nest is easily spotted as a bulky mass of dead sticks, safe from predators in the top of a dead tree or on a rock pinnacle.

You may also see the occasional bald eagle soaring high over the surface of Yellowstone Lake, searching for fish. The adult is easily identified by its black body and white head, and large 6- to 8-foot wingspan. Immature eagles are often misidentified. Look for large, brown birds with whitish markings on the wings and breast. If you are close enough to see the bill, you'll notice that the immature bald eagle has a dark bill compared to the adult's bright yellow one. In more remote areas of Yellowstone Lake, their very large nesting platforms can be seen in the tops of trees.

Of all the birds that migrate to Yellowstone for the summer months, the white pelican is perhaps the most unique. These huge birds are often seen flying in orderly flocks, alternately flapping their wings and gliding. Many times you will see them flying in circles high up in the sky. If you are from a part of the country where brown pelicans reside, you'll notice that the white pelican does not dive for fish as its smaller cousin does. Instead, it settles buoyantly on the water, scooping up fish with its large, yellow bill while swimming along. Look for these birds in large groups resting on the beaches as you approach the inlet of Pelican Creek.

Keep looking into the clear depths below you, too, and you may see some of the large cutthroat trout Yellowstone Lake is famous for.

About 3 miles down the shore you may notice a National Park Service cabin on your left, somewhat hidden in the woods, with Clear Creek entering the lake just before it.

If you are not familiar with the backcountry campsites on Yellowstone Lake, and would like to see what one looks like, the first one along this shore is 0.75 mile ahead, or 3.75 miles from Sedge Bay. If it is not in use at the moment, step ashore and look it over. This is a small site compared to most on the lake, but it has the

Sedge Bay in a placid moment. Afternoon winds can create hazardous paddling conditions on these waters. Exercise caution.

typical campfire area and bear pole for hanging food. A pleasant place along the shore, this may be a good time for a rest or lunch stop. You can also measure your paddling progress and decide whether you want to paddle farther down the shore or turn around at this point. At 6.25 miles from Sedge Bay, another 2.5 miles down the shore, you will reach the second campsite along this stretch of the lake. However far you choose to paddle on this day, you will soon feel very remote from the hustle and bustle of Yellowstone's more developed areas.

Multi-day trips

With 16 backcountry campsites available to paddlers on Shoshone Lake and three dozen sites on Yellowstone Lake, trip options are numerous.

This section describes a variety of trips from two to five days in length. Consider longer trips, too, but keep in mind that the itineraries described here may have to be altered according to campsite availability. Competition for sites can be high, so reserve sites well ahead of your trip, except of course for those that may be reserved only 48 hours ahead of time. Remain flexible in your planning and have second and third choices for your sites. Be sure to consult the park's backcountry campsite planning materials for seasonal closure dates on Yellowstone Lake.

On Yellowstone Lake, as described earlier, there are two launches that provide easy access for overnight trips: Grant Village on the shore of the West Thumb and Sedge Bay on the northeast shore. To reach the more distant and wild southern arms of the lake, you will need a minimum of four days, unless you utilize the boat shuttle service described below.

Trips into Shoshone Lake begin at the Lewis Lake boat launch.

Taking the shuttle

An interesting planning variable to keep in mind for trips on Yellowstone Lake is the park's boat shuttle service. A drop-off at a remote point presents all sorts of new planning possibilities.

Park concessionaires operate motorized boats that can shuttle you and your canoe or kayak to remote points on the lake. The shuttle can reduce your paddling by one to three days, can help you avoid long open-water crossings, and can eliminate the need to retrace your route on a return.

The shuttle serves five points near the arms of the lake: campsites 7L5, 7L6, 7M4, 5L8, and 5E6. See the Yellowstone Lake map (pages 50–51) for these locations.

Most paddlers use round-trip shuttles from Bridge Bay Marina, where the shuttle departs. If you're considering only a pickup or a drop-off, you must arrange your own transportation by road to or from your launch location. For information about the shuttle, call the numbers listed in the Appendix.

Yellowstone Lake's shuttle service uses motorized boats, like the one at the right side of the dock, to haul paddlers and their craft to remote parts of the lake.

SHOSHONE LAKE

Shoshone Lake Trip Planner: Campsite Information

- The following sites are boat access only: 8Q9, 8Q7, 8Q6, 8Q4, 8Q3, 8Q1, 8R1, 8R4, 8S4, 8S5, 8S7, 8T3, 8T5.
- The following sites are accessible to both boaters and hikers: 8S1, 8S2, 8R2.
- The following sites are available for first and last night only: all 8Q sites, and 8S1. These sites are located at convenient distances from the Lewis Lake boat launch and are therefore suitable for most paddlers' itineraries. Due to this, paddlers must move on to other sites the next day to create room for other visitors.
- All sites listed here are limited to eight people. Larger groups may paddle into Shoshone Lake, but they are prohibited from cooking, camping, and congregating together in order to minimize campsite impacts. Prepare and plan for this, and better yet, travel in smaller groups.
- Backcountry site permits must be picked up at the South Entrance, Grant Village, Bridge Bay, or Lake backcountry offices.
- Shoshone Lake does not allow wood fires. Use a gas stove. While charcoal is currently permitted on an experimental basis, it must be in a firepan or grill that is kept in the camp core area and elevated above mineral soil. No wood may be used to supplement the charcoal, and all coals and ashes must be packed out.
- Be sure to request and read park information related to backcountry travel. The Appendix lists addresses and phone numbers for the Central Backcountry Office, which can supply a brochure.

Shoreline Mileages on Shoshone Lake

Mileages are measured clockwise from Shoshone Lake outlet to campsites on the lake. See the Shoshone Lake map (page 64) for locations.

Mileage	Campsite	Mileage	Campsite
0.5	Outlet 8S1	7.25	Hillside 8T3
0.5	Channel 8Q9	12.25	Flat Top 8R4
1.5	Moose Creek Beach 8Q7	13.25	Bluff Top 8R2
2.0	Moose Creek 8Q6	13.75	Windy Point 8R1
2.75	Moose Creek Point #1 8Q4	14.25	North Narrows 8S7
3.25	South Narrows Beach #2 8Q3	15.25	South Grizzly Beach 8S5
3.75	South Narrows Point 8Q1	16.0	North Grizzly Beach 8S4
5.5	Tranquility 8T5	18.0	DeLacy Creek 8S2

7 Lewis Lake to east end of Shoshone Lake

Character: This trip crosses Lewis Lake, travels up the Lewis River Channel and along the south shore of Shoshone Lake to one of several possible campsites.

See map on page 64

Total paddling distance: 14–20 miles, roundtrip.
Average paddling time: 2 days.
Put-in and take-out: Lewis Lake boat launch.
Difficulty: Moderate.
Campsites: Choose any from Outlet 8S1, Channel 8Q9, Moose Creek Beach 8Q7, Moose Creek 8Q6, Moose Creek Point #1 8Q4, South Narrows Beach #2 8Q3, and South Narrows Point 8Q1.
Be aware of: Wind and waves on Lewis and Shoshone lakes, obstacles and current on the Lewis River Channel, precautions for food storage in bear country.
Attractions: Lewis Lake with its sandy beaches and small thermal basin, fishing, wildlife viewing, Shoshone Lake.
Maps: USGS 7.5-minute Mt. Sheridan–WY, Lewis Falls–WY, Shoshone–WY, Geyser Basin–WY.
Use: Moderate to heavy at times in the river channel.
Directions: The Lewis Lake boat launch is on the South Entrance Road 11.1 miles north of Yellowstone's South Entrance and 8.3 miles south of Grant Village Junction where the South Entrance Road is joined by the road to Grant Village.

The paddling: This trip takes you into Shoshone Lake, the largest backcountry lake in the lower 48 states. While a more thorough exploration of this beautiful wilderness setting is only possible with a longer trip, even one night will give you a feel for it. See trips 1 and 2 for details about Lewis Lake and the paddling portion of the Lewis River Channel. This description picks up at the point along the river where, because of the stronger current and shallow water, you must begin to pull, or line, your boat about a mile (more or less, depending on when you decide to stop fighting the current) to Shoshone Lake. Expect strenuous channel conditions as you wade upstream in a cold, swift current and water sometimes waist-deep. The stream is a rock-bottom and fallen trees that often force you out into deeper water. Seasonal fluctuations can be significant with spring conditions being the extreme. Consult the park's backcountry office for expected conditions as you plan your itinerary.

While the place you choose to get out of your boat and plunge into the water to begin lining is up to you, in most cases, it will begin after you have passed several sandbars and small islands above the large rock outcrop. At this point, the stream becomes faster and fills with riffles. Try to disembark on the right bank, where access to the streamside trail is easier for the person not wading.

Wear shoes that protect your feet for the upstream trek. To reduce drag, wear shorts, not long pants. Wet suits or neoprene waders are recommended, especially in the spring when the water is very cold and deep. Do not use hip waders; they can easily fill with water and pull you down.

Shoshone Lake

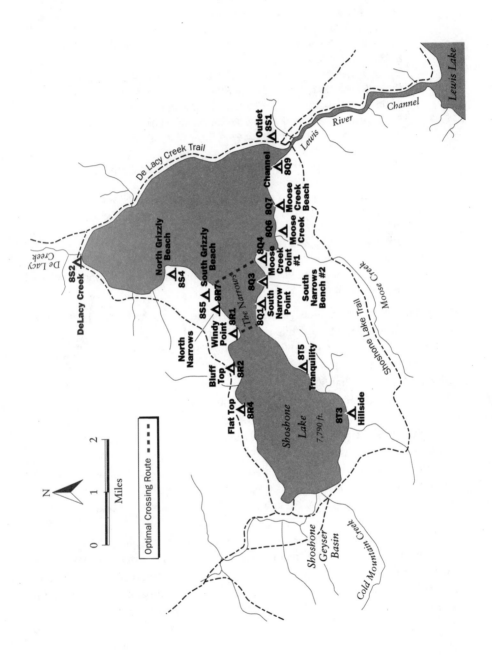

When lining, or pulling, your boat, use a 3/8-inch nylon rope. This size will tangle less and is easier on your hands. Boating gloves, made of neoprene and nylon, can come in handy, too. They protect your skin and keep the hands warm. Attach a minimum of 25 feet of rope to the bow of your boat so that you can work your way around rocks and fallen trees.

Some people prefer to use a rope at least 75 feet long, and attached bow and stern. With this arrangement and with some practice, you can literally "fly" the boat out and back in the current and around rocks and fallen trees by moving the line through your hands, while remaining closer to the bank. You'll still find, however, that fallen trees will force you to wade in the water much of the time. Consult a good canoeing manual to learn the fine points of lining. It's not quite as easy as it may sound.

Depending on physical strength and condition, this upstream part of the trip can be quite wearing. Take your time, resting and warming up on the bank as necessary. On cool, rainy days, this upstream effort can be even more challenging. Give yourself at least an hour and a half to complete this leg of the trip. Before you know it the stream will begin to meander some, and a glance ahead will soon provide your first view of Shoshone Lake.

If you made your way up the right bank where the going is easier, you will come out on a large gravel beach. This is a great time and place to rest, snack some, and change clothes if necessary before heading on to camp.

There are several sites that may be reserved within a reasonable distance from this point. Campsite 8S1 is located almost immediately to the right on the far east shore of the lake. Just a short paddle along the left, or west, shore lies site 8Q9, hidden in the trees. There are five more sites, 8Q7, 8Q6, 8Q4, 8Q3, and 8Q1, spread out along the next 3 miles of shoreline up to the "narrows" of the lake. Sites 8Q7, 8Q6, and 8Q1 are near the beach, while 8Q4 and 8Q3 are situated more in the woods and higher on shore. Each site has a pit toilet and a bear pole for hanging your food, beverages, cooking gear, and any scented items while you are away from camp or sleeping. Please minimize your impact by practicing leave-no-trace techniques.

When you depart on day two and have worked your way along the shore to the river, you can look forward to a fun float down to Lewis Lake. You only need to steer much of the way, beginning to paddle near the large rock outcrop. Watch for other paddlers negotiating their way downstream and give them plenty of room. Other paddlers may be trudging upstream as you did yesterday. Give them encouragement!

A word to the wise: When you enter Lewis Lake, assess wave conditions carefully. It is recommended that you paddle along the right, or west shore, back to the boat launch to avoid dangerous conditions out on the lake, especially along the windward north shore. Relax and do not take chances by rushing to the boat launch.

8   Lewis Lake to Bluff Top

Character: This trip explores the south shore and part of the north shore of Shoshone Lake, giving

See map on page 64

you a good wilderness experience, with an opportunity to spend at least some time in the Shoshone Geyser Basin. Two very different camps, one at Moose Creek and one at Bluff Top, are used.

Total paddling distance: Approximately 29 miles.

Put-in and take-out: Lewis Lake boat launch.

Difficulty: Moderate to difficult.

Campsites: Moose Creek 8Q6, Moose Creek Beach 8Q7, Bluff Top 8R2.

Be aware of: Afternoon winds and accompanying waves, thin crust and hot water in thermal basin, precautions for food storage in bear country.

Attractions: Pristine waters, Lewis River Channel, Shoshone Geyser Basin, bird watching, wildlife viewing, fishing.

Maps: USGS 7.5-minute Mt. Sheridan–WY, Lewis Falls–WY, Craig Pass–WY, Shoshone Geyser Basin–WY.

Use: Moderate to heavy in the river channel.

Directions: The Lewis Lake boat launch is on the South Entrance Road, 11.1 miles north of Yellowstone's South Entrance and 8.3 miles south of the Grant Village Junction, where the South Entrance Road is joined by the road to Grant Village.

The paddling: This trip can be considered strenuous because it crosses Lewis Lake, travels up the Lewis River Channel, and spends two nights on Shoshone Lake at two different camps with time to explore the Shoshone Geyser Basin. You must have early starts, strong paddling skills, and favorable conditions. For more detail on Lewis Lake and the Lewis River Channel, refer to trips 1, 2, and 7. After a break on the beach as you enter Shoshone Lake, head along the south shore. Your first night will be spent at one of two sites about 1.5 miles away, Moose Creek (8Q6) or Moose Creek Beach (8Q7). Both sites are located in scattered trees and very near the adjacent beaches, with great views of the lake looking north. Moose occasionally wander into the large marshy area behind the sites. Moose Creek creates the marsh as it enters the lake.

Moose are the largest member of the deer family, weighing as much as 1,000 pounds, occasionally more. Adults can stand more than 7 feet tall at the shoulder. Like all members of the deer family, only males grow antlers, which are dropped annually. This is particularly amazing when you consider that a large moose may have antlers as wide as 6 feet across.

Moose can be found from low elevation sagebrush to high altitude timberline habitats and are very often seen in wet areas eating willow, shrubs, and water plants. Interestingly, moose prefer elevations above 9,000 feet in winter, where they feed primarily on conifers. While they have very long legs, easing movement in deep snow, they prefer the thick needle canopy of conifers which catches snow,

Canoes pass rock ledges on Shoshone Lake.

thereby reducing snow depths and making travel easier.

If you are paddling in September or October, use caution around moose since males are in rut and enthusiastically seeking females; they may become quite aggressive. Unlike elk, the male moose does not assemble a harem, remaining content with a single female that he stays with for ten days or so, until moving on to another female.

On your second day, head to site 8R2, Bluff Top, a beautiful site situated in the woods on a high point overlooking the lake. As you travel along the south shore portion of this 9-mile paddle, you float by heavily wooded shorelines. There are five sites along this stretch where you may see other campers. If the sites are unoccupied, stop and take a look for future reference.

About two-thirds along the way you come to the Shoshone Geyser Basin, tucked in a bay on the very northwest edge of the lake. The basin is well worth as long a visit as your schedule allows. Unlike more accessible basins in the park, this one can only be reached by water or a rather long hike. Although you will more than likely encounter other visitors, it remains largely untouched by humans. To grasp the significance of this basin, read T. Scott Bryan's *The Geysers of Yellowstone* (1995), in which 27 pages are devoted to this basin alone. Bryan states that Shoshone "is one of the most important thermal areas in the world, even though its major portion measures only 1,600 by 800 feet. The basin may contain as many as eighty geysers, perhaps more than any single place on earth other than the remainder of Yellowstone and the Valley of Geysers on Russia's Kamchatka Peninsula." It's a backcountry privilege to explore this undeveloped basin without fences, board-

A serene Shoshone Lake, viewed from the Bluff Top campsite.

walks, or signs but with the privilege comes the responsibility to use great care so that you do not damage the features. Leave no evidence of your visit to this special place.

Stay on the paths, away from the scalding hot water, which can severely burn the skin. While many visitors to Yellowstone are fearful of grizzly bear attacks, there have been many more deaths from hot water than bears. Most thermal features in the park are hotter than 150 degrees, and many are at or above 200 degrees. Remember that water boils at 198 degrees at Yellowstone's elevation. Over the years many visitors have been severely injured or killed as a result of accidental contact with thermal waters. A misstep may be fatal. Take for example the story of a 9-year-old boy who lost his balance on a boardwalk, perhaps momentarily "blinded" by steam. Falling into the 200 degree water, the boy attempted a few strokes then sank out of sight. The next day, eight pounds of flesh, bones, and clothing were recovered from the pool.

This sad story is not an unnecessary exaggeration of the risks of travel in thermal areas. It can happen anytime and anywhere thermal water exists. Use great caution in the thermal landscape, stay on established paths, and always keep children within arms reach.

National Park Service regulations prohibit paddlers from leaving bear attractants, such as food, unattended in boats on the beach. Someone from your party must remain at the boats during the time you are exploring the basin.

Once you leave the basin, continue your paddle about 3.0 miles to Bluff Top. Keep a lookout for the orange site marker, set back from the open water on a small, protected beach. This is the landing area. The large, flat, wooded site is located on the bluff to the right up a steep, short trail. While not as handy to your boat and gear as other sites in the area, the higher location offers a wonderful view of the lake. There is also a trail to the geyser basin from this site.

The last day is your return to Lewis Lake. From Bluff Top, paddle east 0.75 mile along the shore to where the lake narrows and make the 0.5 mile, 15- to 20-minute crossing to the south shore, then retrace the 3 miles to the Lewis River Channel. Remember that any lake crossing increases your risks and is potentially hazardous. Start early in the day and use good judgment to evaluate conditions. If the winds rise, get to shore as fast as you can and wait for calmer conditions to cross. The float down the river is quick and fun. Watch for rocks and trees in the river and in an hour or so you are back on Lewis Lake. Generally you will be returning to the boat launch in the afternoon so you can expect the typical buildup of wind and waves.

A word to the wise: Stay near the west shore, resisting the urge to save time by crossing Lewis Lake in rough conditions. It saves little time and puts you at far greater risk.

9   Lewis Lake to South Grizzly Beach

Character: This trip is similar in length to trip 8, except that you paddle considerably longer the first day. You'll see more of the shoreline and still have an opportunity to visit Shoshone Geyser Basin.

See map on page 64

Total paddling distance: Approximately 27 miles.
Suggested time: 3 days.
Put-in and take-out: Lewis Lake boat launch.
Difficulty: Difficult.
Campsites: Tranquility 8T5 and South Grizzly Beach 8S5. (Tranquility sometimes closed in spring due to high water at the landing.)
Be aware of: Afternoon winds and accompanying waves, thin crust and hot water in thermal basin, precautions for food storage in bear country.
Attractions: Lewis River Channel, Shoshone Geyser Basin, moose, bird watching, fishing.
Maps: USGS 7.5-minute Mt. Sheridan–WY, Lewis Falls–WY, Craig Pass–WY, Shoshone Geyser Basin–WY.
Use: Moderate to heavy in the river channel.
Directions: The Lewis Lake boat launch is on the South Entrance Road 11.1 miles north of Yellowstone's South Entrance and 8.3 miles south of Grant Village Junction, where the South Entrance Road is joined by the road to Grant Village.

The paddling: This trip is very strenuous and should be attempted only by experienced paddlers. You embark from Lewis Lake boat launch, as in all overnight trips

A visitor looks across Shoshone Lake from the Shoshone Geyser Basin.

into Shoshone Lake, and make your way across Lewis Lake and up the Lewis River Channel to the beach at the entrance to Shoshone Lake. (Consult "The paddling" in trips 2 and 7 on how to reach the beach.) From there, you start the 5.5 mile paddle west along the south shore to the Tranquility campsite (8T5), making for a 12-mile total for the day. A trip of this length is quite strenuous, and this one includes the upstream effort of the river channel. Additionally, in the afternoon, especially west of "The Narrows," you can expect difficult lake conditions. You'll likely be paddling into the wind. Tranquility, a heavily wooded camp, will be a welcome site! The landing area is small and windward, which complicates getting out of your boat and unloading gear, but the view from the site will make your labors worth your while. You may be able to see steam rising from Shoshone Geyser Basin to the west. Beautiful sunsets are common here, too.

Next day you continue around the shoreline clockwise. While this day of paddling is shorter than the day before, it still takes three to five hours and you may want to allow time to explore the geyser basin (described in trip 8). When you leave the thermal area and begin to head east toward camp, you may experience wind and waves, most often coming from the west.

A word to the wise: Paddling with a strong wind at your back can be difficult, even though you may find yourself being carried along. Use care so that waves do not turn your craft broadside to the waves. In strong winds, this position can easily lead to a capsize.

Your second day of paddling ends at South Grizzly Beach (8S5), located 1.5 miles east of the "The Narrows" and about 10 miles along the shore from Tranquility.

South Grizzly Beach is a flat, wooded site, set back from the lake by a long, wide beach. The beach narrows north of the camp and is a great place to go exploring for tracks of other creatures that use the area. To help identify animal signs, bring along *Scats and Tracks of the Rocky Mountains* by James Halfpenny (Falcon, 1998).

If conditions are calm enough when you break camp on day three, you can make a 1-mile crossing to the south shore of the lake, but do so early enough to avoid possible afternoon wind and waves. This crossing is recommended only under the calmest of conditions. Use your best judgment and check the sky for signs of inclement weather. If you proceed, head for the point of land to the south and east. Once you reach the point, you will be about 2.5 miles to the Lewis River Channel, which you labored up three days ago. If water conditions or weather are such that you are uncomfortable with the 1-mile crossing, paddle clockwise the 8 miles of shoreline to the Lewis River Channel outlet. While this paddle adds considerably to your day, it is well worth it if the risks of crossing are high. You can also opt to backtrack along the shoreline and cross at "The Narrows." Whatever route you choose, make it safe; then have fun and enjoy the almost effortless 3.5-

The South Grizzly Beach campsite on Shoshone Lake.

mile trip down the river channel to Lewis Lake. When you get there, paddle with caution, near shore, the remaining distance to the boat launch.

10 Lewis Lake to DeLacy Creek

See map on page 64

Character: Of the three-day trips on Shoshone Lake described in this book, this one involves the most paddling. It follows the entire shoreline, including the usual crossing of Lewis Lake and the upstream trek of the Lewis River Channel. If you want to explore all of this backcountry lake in a strenuous three days, this trip's for you.

Total paddling distance: 35 miles.

Suggested time: 3 days.

Put-in and take-out: Lewis Lake boat launch.

Difficulty: Difficult.

Campsites: Hillside 8T3, DeLacy Creek 8S2.

Be aware of: Afternoon wind and accompanying waves, thin crust and hot water in thermal basin, precautions for food storage in bear country.

Attractions: Lewis River Channel, Shoshone Geyser Basin, bird watching, wildlife viewing, fishing.

Maps: USGS 7.5-minute Mt. Sheridan–WY, Lewis Falls–WY, Craig Pass–WY, Shoshone Geyser Basin–WY.

Use: Moderate to heavy in the river channel.

Directions: The Lewis Lake boat launch is on the South Entrance Road 11.1 miles north of Yellowstone's South Entrance and 8.3 miles south of Grant Village Junction, where the South Entrance Road is joined by the road to Grant Village.

Shoshone Creek and thermal features of Shoshone Geyser Basin.

The paddling: Getting across Lewis Lake and up the Lewis River Channel are covered in trips 2 and 7. Selected segments of paddling Shoshone Lake are described in trips 8 and 9. Review those descriptions for details of what to expect on this challenging trip and use great caution. Remember that anything other than ideal weather conditions will add effort, time, and risk to an already strenuous itinerary.

After paddling the 7 miles of lake and river to reach Shoshone Lake, continue another 7.5 miles along the south shore to Hillside camp (8T3), the last site on the south side of the lake. Look for the site up among the trees. It has a wonderful view of the entire west end of the lake, including glimpses of the Shoshone Geyser Basin. This first day of paddling is an especially long one, so get an early start and be prepared for the inevitable strong afternoon headwinds as you paddle westward on Shoshone Lake.

Day two is another long paddle, with a highly recommended side trip to explore the geyser basin (described in trip 8, page 66). The camp at DeLacy Creek (8S2) is about 11 miles away, so an early start is mandatory if you are to spend any time at the basin. From the geyser basin you have about a 9-mile paddle to camp. This north end of the lake is nearly all beach, making it a wonderful place to camp. The trail that follows the east and north shore of the lake comes near this camp, making 8S2 accessible to hikers.

When you depart on your third day, you have a 4.5-mile paddle to the river channel.

Landing at Shoshone Geyser Basin.

A word to the wise: The shoreline along this stretch of the lake is rather steep, wooded, and rocky, making it largely impossible to beach your boat. Broadside waves can build up quite high along this shore due to prevailing winds coming across the entire 9-mile length of the lake. Consider this when planning the first part of your third day's paddle.

Within a couple of hours you are floating leisurely 3.5 miles downstream on your way to Lewis Lake and then another 3.5 miles to the boat launch. Resist the temptation to cut directly across the lake to the launch. Use care and take your time by following the west shore.

YELLOWSTONE LAKE

Shoreline Mileages on Yellowstone Lake

Mileages are measured counterclockwise from the Grant Village boat launch. See the Yellowstone Lake map (pages 50–51) for locations.

Miles	Campsite	Miles	Campsite
7.0	Breeze Point North 7L1	19.5	Plover Point 7M4
8.0	Breeze Bay South 7L2	20.5	Plover Bay 7M5
9.0	Ravine 7L4	22.0	South Arm 7M6
10.0	Wolf Bay 7L5	23.0	South Arm 7M7
12.0	Eagle Bay 7L6	24.0	South Arm 7M9
13.5	Bodego Bay 7L7	25.5	Gowdy Camp 7N2
15.0	Flat Mountain Arm North 7L8	26.5	Southwest Bay 7N4
15.5	Flat Mountain Arm South 7L9	28.0	Peale Island 7N6
17.7	Flat Mountain Bay 7M3		

■11■ Grant Village to Wolf Point

See map on pages 50–51

Character: This trip starts at Grant Village and follows the south shore of the West Thumb, past Breeze Point, into Yellowstone Lake, and ending at Wolf Point and its protected bay.
Total paddling distance: 20 miles.
Suggested time: 2 days.
Put-in and take-out: Grant Village boat launch.
Difficulty: Moderate.

Campsites: Breeze Point North 7L1, Breeze Bay South 7L2, Ravine 7L4, Wolf Bay 7L5.

Be aware of: Afternoon winds and accompanying waves, precautions for food storage in bear country.

Attractions: Views of West Thumb Geyser Basin, beaches at Breeze Point, views of the Absaroka Range to the west, bird watching (especially water birds, bald eagles, and ospreys), fishing, and Wolf Bay and Wolf Point.

Maps: USGS 7.5-minute West Thumb–WY, and Dot Island–WY.

Use: Light.

Directions: The Grant Village boat launch is located by turning east at Grant Village Junction, 2.5 miles south of West Thumb, 8.3 miles north of Lewis Lake Campground, and 19.4 miles north of the South Entrance. After the turn to Grant Village, drive 1 mile to the first intersection and turn right at the Hamilton Store. Follow the signs down to the marina. It is most convenient to park at the right (south) end of the parking area.

The paddling: This trip follows the south shore of the West Thumb and rounds Breeze Point before entering Yellowstone Lake proper. The campsite at Wolf Point is the 10-mile destination, but there are three other campsites along this route, spaced about every mile, that you may use to make the trip shorter. Trip 4 describes the route from the boat launch to Breeze Point, about 6 miles of paddling and more than halfway to the destination. The beach area at the point is a pleasant place to rest and enjoy the scenery, including the views of the Absaroka Range to the east across Yellowstone Lake. You can also see Dot and Frank islands.

Paddling around the point you'll notice that much of the forest has been burned in the past, evidence of the massive fires that moved through this area in 1988. Some people are alarmed by the changes in the Yellowstone landscape wrought by the fires. To them, it seems ruined or damaged. It is important to remember, though, that landscapes, with their various communities of plants and animals, change over time, being slowly replaced by subsequent, or successive, communities. These changes, or successions, lead to a diverse mosaic of communities that constitute the landscape before you. After a series of successions, a community of plants and animals will eventually stabilize, or climax, with little or no change taking place. This final, or late succession is based primarily on the climate of the location and will only begin to change again when disturbed in some way.

Fire is one of the most common, healthy, and natural ways in which a community can be disturbed. Once a fire moves through a landscape, it creates many opportunities for change. In short, a door is opened in the more homogenous ecosystem that existed before the fire, allowing for greater ecological diversity to enter. With the increase in diversity comes an increase in ecosystem stability. A relatively simple landscape, supporting fewer wildlife species, is replaced by a more vital and diverse landscape.

With the burning and falling of trees, forests open up so that greater sunlight reaches the soil surface. This leads to the growth of varied ground cover plants, which leads in turn to an increase in smaller animals inhabiting the area. With smaller animals living there, different predators enter and occupy the renewed landscape. Dead trees attract insects, and populations of insectivorous birds, such as woodpeckers, increase. Landscapes that are returned to an earlier successional stage through fire often offer improved elk and deer habitat, too. Aspen and willow thrive in the aftermath of fire, thus providing more food for beaver.

While the fires in Yellowstone were dramatic examples of what can happen following years of fire suppression, the result has been a rejuvenated landscape, offering much more not only for the park's inhabitants, but also for its human visitors.

The dead trees have become popular nesting and roosting places for ospreys and eagles. There can be quite a few of both these birds of prey in the area so keep your eyes focused toward shore and overhead in the dead snags near the shore. Be aware that dead trees can be a hazard in and around camp. Try to select a tent location that is not at risk of falling trees.

The first site you come upon, Breeze Point North (7L1), about a mile from Breeze Point (7 miles from Grant Village), is a very private and protected site in the woods to the right in a small bay created behind a gravel beach and spit. Look for the orange diamond that marks the site, as with all sites on the lake. While many of the trees are dead in this area, there is a nice grove of conifers at the camp.

About two-thirds of the way down Breeze Bay, the larger bay that sweeps to the south, is the second camp, Breeze Bay South (7L2). It is hidden in the woods near shore with a gravel beach on which to take out your boat. As with almost all sites on this lake, this one is very private.

As you paddle away from the bay and continue on around the shoreline, look for interesting caves in the volcanic rock cliffs along this section, and continue to look for water birds and ospreys in the trees overhead. About 1 mile from the last site, on the shoreline in the dead trees, look for a horizontal bear pole, indicating you have arrived at the third site along this section. This is Ravine (7L4), a large flat site, high enough above the water that you gain a new perspective of the view toward Frank Island. The take-out is just to the left where a small creek enters the lake.

Paddling on around this large promontory you soon come upon a long gravel beach and sandbar, or spit, stretching down to the south. This is Wolf Point, near your destination. You have traveled 10 miles by water. Pausing along the spit, you can see your site, Wolf Bay (7L5), back to the right in the grove of conifers along the grassy shoreline. You need to paddle around the end of the spit to enter Wolf Bay. This site is unique in that it is one of three that has a boat dock used for the park shuttle service and for private motorboat operators. One canoe or kayak party at a time is permitted here.

This bay is rather large and protected from many of the winds that move through. The shoreline is a great place to explore from land or by water. After camp is set up, walk inland among the burned over trees, enjoying the new forest that is springing up in the aftermath of the 1988 fires. The wildflowers can be wonderful, and keep a lookout for a variety of birds, including the many wood-peckers that feed on the insects in the dead trees. Note that this site, as with many on Yellowstone Lake, does not permit travel by land from camp between May 15 and July 14 to minimize possible interference with grizzly bears during this impor-tant time of feeding on cutthroat trout. From your site look to the southeast. The relatively high point off to the left, beyond Snipe Point immediately across the bay, is The Promontory, the northern end of land dividing the two lower arms of Yellowstone Lake. Frank Island is located due east of your camp.

In preparation for your return to Grant Village on the second day, plan for a head wind and waves as you cross the West Thumb. They can result in a stressful ending to your trip if you have not given yourself enough time. Stay close to shore.

12 Sedge Bay to Meadow Creek

Overview: This trip explores the lake's eastern shore, using one of three possible backcountry campsite destinations.

See map on pages 50–51

Total paddling distance: Up to 14 miles.
Suggested time: 2 days.
Put-in and take-out: Sedge Bay boat launch.
Difficulty: Moderate.
Campsites: Midshore 5H1, Park Point North 5E9, or Park Point South 5E8.
Be aware of: Afternoon winds and accompanying waves, precautions for food storage in bear country.
Attractions: Remote paddling, bird watching (especially waterfowl).
Maps: USGS 7.5-minute Lake Butte–WY, Frank Island–WY.
Use: Light.
Directions: Sedge Bay is located at the northeast corner of Yellowstone Lake, just southeast of the more prominent Mary Bay. The Sedge Bay boat launch can be reached by driving approximately 8 miles east from Fishing Bridge to the last parking area before the road goes uphill and inland from the shoreline. Look for a pullout on the right between the road and the shore.

The paddling: Review trip 6 for a detailed description of this route along the east shore of Yellowstone Lake. There are three backcountry campsites that you can choose from. The first site you come to is Midshore (5H1), 3.75 miles, or 1.5 to 2 hours, down the shore. It is a small, but wooded and grassy site, capable of hold-ing two small tents. There is a long gravel beach just a few feet from camp and a nice campfire area with a beautiful view of the lake to the west, including a possible sunset if you are lucky.

The next site, Park Point South (5E8), is 6.25 miles from Sedge Bay, and 2.5 miles from the first site. You know you are nearing it when you see a very large

The volcanic rock along the eastern shore of Yellowstone Lake offers an interesting backdrop.

grassy meadow reaching up to the left across the hillside. There is a somewhat rough gravel-and-rock beach stretching along the entire length of the hill and just around the bend is the site marker. After landing, wander up the hillside to where it flattens out and you will find the campsite, fire pit, and bear pole. Tall meadow grasses and wildflowers surround the site, located among mature conifers. The site is far above the lake, giving you vast panoramic views to the west. You can see the sweeping, wooded shorelines that lead to the upper entrances of both southern arms of the lake, with The Promontory, the rugged tip of a peninsula, between them. Frank Island is due east. This site has the farthest-reaching views of any on the lake.

Paralleling the shoreline and just back in the woods is the Thorofare Trail, a popular backpacking and horsepacking route that follows the entire east shore of Yellowstone Lake. If you want to stretch your legs, you can easily find this trail by walking directly back from camp and then heading north or south on the trail. Off-trail travel away from camp is not permitted from April 1 to July 14 to minimize conflicts with bears feeding on spawning trout.

A short 0.75 mile further down the shore is site 5E8, located just past the inlet of Meadow Creek. As with the other sites along this shoreline, you locate the camp by looking for a long gravel beach and an orange site marker. This is another terrific site with plenty of room, a large campfire area, and great views across the lake. By walking back in the woods along Meadow Creek and scrambling around down trees, you come to a very large, and sometimes wet, meadow and the Thorofare Trail. There is another short walk south through the woods paralleling the beach that works its way around trees and rocks into a wide meadow that rises above a rocky cliff at the water's edge. The cliff edge offers a sweeping view of the lake country beyond. Note that walking away from camp, as with most of the lake shoreline, is not permitted between April 1 and July 14.

A word to the wise: Plan to depart for your return trip early to avoid the typical buildup of large waves in the afternoon hours.

13 Grant Village to Bodego Bay

Character: This trip is a wonderful way to explore the south shore of the West Thumb and the long, sandy beaches at Breeze Point. It gives you just a hint of the seclusion offered by the Flat Mountain Arm.

See map on pages 50–51

Total paddling distance: 27 miles.
Suggested time: 3 days.
Put-in and take-out: Grant Village boat launch.
Difficulty: Moderate to difficult.
Campsites: Breeze Bay South 7L2, Bodego Bay 7L7.
Be aware of: Afternoon winds and accompanying waves, precautions for food storage in bear country.
Attractions: Sandy beaches (especially at Breeze Point and Wolf Point), bird watching, a glimpse into the Flat Mountain Arm.
Maps: USGS 7.5-minute West Thumb–WY, Dot Island–WY, Mt. Sheridan–WY, Heart Lake–WY.
Use: Light to moderate.
Directions: The Grant Village boat launch is located by turning east at Grant Village Junction, 2.5 miles south of West Thumb, 8.3 miles north of Lewis Lake Campground, or 19.4 miles north of the South Entrance. After the turn to Grant Village, drive 1 mile to the first intersection and turn right at the Hamilton Store. Follow the signs down to the marina. It is most convenient to park at the right (south) end of the parking area.

The paddling: This trip offers a big lake paddling experience with a look at the upper reaches of the Flat Mountain Arm, the smallest of Yellowstone Lake's three arms. Over this three-day trip, you stay at two different campsites, the second of which is in the northeastern portion of the arm. Review trip 4 for details of the West Thumb portion of this trip and the initial paddle into Yellowstone Lake. When departing from the launch at Grant Village, be sure to look north to the thermal basin. If the morning is cool, large amounts of steam will be rising and lit by the sun rising in the east. Waters are generally calm in the morning and the 5-mile paddle around West Thumb can be very relaxing and a nice warm-up.

As described previously, once you begin to pass east through the narrower section of the lake, the shoreline begins to change to beaches, perfect for taking a break. When you get to Breeze Point, the long sand spit extending into the lake, you have paddled 6 miles and are about 2 miles from Breeze Bay South (7L2),

The Bodego Bay campsite on Flat Mountain Arm of Yellowstone Lake.

your first camp. Trip 8 gives greater detail about paddling Breeze Bay. Breeze Bay South is a secluded, wooded site with a small, gravel beach on which to take out your boat and open woods behind. Its location in the bay, and on the west shore, keep it fairly protected from prevailing winds. Many paddlers choose to cut across this bay in calm conditions, giving you even greater privacy at this site. You have good views of the lake and mountains to the north, and the morning sun will come into your camp from the hillside behind.

You can start day two at a leisurely pace since your next site, Bodego Bay (7L7), is only 5.5 miles away. The short paddle to this destination leaves you time to explore the beaches at Wolf Point, a couple of miles down the shore, or to paddle further into Flat Mountain Arm after you have set up camp. This is a great camp location, up in the woods, with nice beaches to relax on, while you enjoy the panoramic view of the lake. The morning sun reaches this camp early. The fires of 1988 had some impact on this area, but the forest is recovering nicely, leaving an open, spacious feeling with lots of ground cover. Watch your step. A careless walker can cause dead standing trees to fall.

On your third day, you return the way you came, paddling the 13.5 miles back to Grant Village.

A word to the wise: Plan on a tough return paddle, at least 6 to 7 hours, into headwinds and accompanying waves once you reach Breeze Bay and West Thumb. Stay close to the southern shore of West Thumb. Leave early to avoid rough water conditions in the afternoon hours. If stormy weather prevails, be prepared to land until it improves.

In order to avoid this last paddle, you can arrange ahead of time to have a shuttle boat pick you up, but the boat will take you to Bridge Bay Marina, where you'll have to have transportation back to Grant Village. If you choose to use the shuttle, the nearest pickup is at the Eagle Bay campsite (7L6), a dock site on the north side of the bay, 3.5 miles north of your current camp at Bodego Bay. Check with the shuttle concessionaire for the schedule. The phone number is listed in the Appendix.

14 Grant Village to Flat Mountain Bay

Character: This trip takes you from Grant Village around the south shore of West Thumb and

See map on pages 50–51

through the entire Flat Mountain Arm, staying at three different camps, before ending on the fourth day with a long paddle back to Grant Village.

Total paddling distance: 36 miles.
Suggested time: 4 days.
Put-in and take-out: Grant Village boat launch.
Difficulty: Moderate to difficult.
Campsites: Breeze Bay South 7L2, Flat Mountain Arm North 7L8, Flat Mountain Bay 7M3.
Be aware of: Afternoon winds and accompanying waves, precautions for food storage in bear country.
Attractions: Pristine paddling in the intimate setting of the Flat Mountain Arm, bird watching, some hiking, fishing.
Maps: USGS 7.5-minute West Thumb–WY, Dot Island–WY, Mt.

The tortured rock shoreline of Flat Mountain Arm.

Sheridan–WY, Heart Lake–WY.

Use: Light to moderate.

Directions: The Grant Village boat launch is located by turning east at Grant Village Junction, 2.5 miles south of West Thumb, 8.3 miles north of Lewis Lake Campground, or 19.4 miles north of the South Entrance. After the turn to Grant Village, drive 1 mile to the first intersection and turn right at the Hamilton Store. Follow the signs down to the marina. It is most convenient to park at the right (south) end of the parking area.

The paddling: This trip is a four-day exploration of much of the west side of Yellowstone Lake, including two nights camping in the beautiful, secluded Flat Mountain Arm. You move each day, staying at three different sites along the way. You can paddle the first day with some leisure, knowing that the first camp, Breeze Bay South (7L2), is just 8 miles down the shore (about three to five hours). Depart early enough, though, to avoid the buildup of large waves in the afternoon. For a description of this 8-mile trip, refer to trip 4. For a description of the Breeze Bay South site, see trip 8 or 13.

The second night's camp is 7 miles from Breeze Bay South. This is a relatively short paddle, and since your first site is so beautiful and secluded, take your time departing. Once you head off, take time to wander around Wolf Point and Wolf Bay, 2 miles farther down the shoreline. Get out at Wolf Point and explore this wonderful sand spit. Watch for ospreys, too, but stay away if they are nearby. Ospreys in Yellowstone tolerate little disturbance from humans. When paddling, keep your distance from osprey nests; move out into safe open water. If you are close enough that the bird seems intensely focused on you, back off. Adults kept away from nests due to repeated human interference may fail to produce young and are prevented from shading eggs or young from the sun. Birds perched in trees away from nests are resting or in search of fish. Give them the space they need to care for themselves and their nestlings.

Eagle Bay, another 2 miles along the shore, has a nice site you may want to check out for a future stay.

At this point, you're only 3 miles from your second camp, Flat Mountain Arm North (7L8), which is up from the shore in the trees on the north side of the arm. As is the case with many sites on Yellowstone Lake, this one is closed from May 15 to July 14 to allow grizzly bears in the area to feed undisturbed on spawning trout. From here, you can look up and down the arm. When you get there, you'll probably have plenty of time to get out for a paddle, to fish, or to set up camp and relax during the afternoon.

Day three is a wonderful paddle around the Flat Mountain Arm. This arm, compared to Yellowstone Lake's other two arms, is small and intimate. The arm is about 3 miles long and from 0.25 to 0.5 mile wide. Since your final night's camp is another 7-mile paddle, you have time to explore the beaches and rocky shoreline of the entire arm. While there are no designated trails in this area, the remote end

A campsite take-out on Flat Mountain Arm.

of the arm is a great place to beach your boat and go hiking. The woods are quite open, with meadows scattered throughout. Many people choose to spend much of their time fishing the clear water for the cutthroat trout Yellowstone Lake is famous for.

Your last camp is Flat Mountain Bay (7M3) at the far east end of the arm, tucked back in the corner of the bay. Like other sites on this arm, it is wooded and private, with a wonderful view of the lake. Before turning in for the night, take some time to consider the long 15-mile paddle awaiting you the next day. When you leave camp in the morning, you have two choices: to head north and across the mouth of the bay, or to head about 1 mile west down the arm to a narrower crossing.

A word to the wise: The National Park Service wisely recommends against open-water crossings. The mouth of the arm is about 0.75 mile, 30 minutes or more of paddling, and far enough to leave you in a dangerous spot if a storm builds up. Use caution in assessing conditions. Use good sense with this decision and do not take chances. If water conditions are questionable, paddling the longer, but safer route, down and across the narrower portion of the arm, is much wiser.

Once you reach the north side of the mouth of the arm, retrace your steps around Eagle Bay and on to West Thumb. Rest often along the way and plan for headwinds and possibly for large waves as you paddle in Breeze Bay and across the Thumb to Grant Village. Stay safely close to shore along the way.

15 Grant Village to Plover Point

Character: This trip covers most of the western part of Yellowstone Lake, including a paddle to *See map on pages 50–51* the most remote stretches of the South Arm. You will see about one-fourth of the lake's shoreline.

Total paddling distance: 50 miles.

Suggested time: 5 days.

Put-in and take-out: Grant Village boat launch.

Difficulty: Moderate to difficult.

Campsites: Eagle Bay 7L6, South Arm 7M9, Chipmunk Creek Outlet 5L3, Plover Point 7M4.

Be aware of: Wind and waves, especially in the afternoon; precautions for food storage in bear country.

Attractions: Pristine, big lake paddling, long sandy beaches, South Arm, wildlife viewing, bird watching, fishing.

Maps: USGS 7.5-minute West Thumb–WY, Dot Island–WY, Mt. Sheridan–WY, Heart Lake–WY.

Use: Moderate.

Directions: The Grant Village boat launch is located by turning east at Grant Village Junction, 2.5 miles south of West Thumb, 8.3 miles north of Lewis Lake Campground, or 19.4 miles north of the South Entrance. After the turn to Grant Village, drive 1 mile to the first intersection and turn right at the Hamilton Store. Follow the signs down to the marina. It is most convenient to park at the right (south) end of the parking area.

Peale Island is reflected in the calm waters of the South Arm of Yellowstone Lake.

The paddling: This 5-day trip averages 10 miles a day as you paddle through the West Thumb, into Yellowstone Lake, to the farthest reaches of the South Arm, and back to Grant Village. Read descriptions for trips 4, 11, 13, and 14 for details about the first day of paddling. Eagle Bay (7L6), your first camp, is 12 shoreline miles from Grant Village, making for a fairly long first day on the water. This large, two-site area has a dock and may be used by up to three parties, one of which must be self-contained for offshore camping, either moored or docked. Only one self-propelled party is allowed. This site is also one of five used by the park's shuttle service for pickups and drop-offs. This site has more activity than most in the area, but it is well maintained.

Paddling to your second campsite can be a much easier 7.5 miles, but this depends to some extent on weather conditions and whether you cut across the Flat Mountain Arm, a risky proposition at times. If you depart camp early enough, and water conditions are calm, you may choose to make the 0.75-mile crossing of the arm at its mouth, shortening the day's paddle considerably. If unsettled weather or winds suggest it would be unwise to attempt the crossing, play it safe and paddle about halfway up the Flat Mountain Arm where you can gain a shorter crossing. This could add up to 3 miles of paddling, but it is well worth it if conditions for the wider crossing appear unsafe.

A word to the wise: It's best to be conservative when deciding to cross or not to cross. Weather in these mountains changes rapidly and can catch paddlers offguard during a long crossing. Don't take chances.

Once you reach the large point of land between Flat Mountain Arm and South Arm, you have paddled about 2.5 miles and have 5 miles remaining to South Arm campsite 7M9. When you round the point and head south into the arm, look for a large, white marker to the right on the west shore. This marks the point south of which motorboat operators must limit their speed to 5 miles per hour. The boundary of the 5-mph zone stretches from this marker to a similar marker on the east shore. It is shown on maps as a line drawn through the northernmost tip of the Promontory (see map on pages 50, 51).

South Arm campsite 7M9 is on the south edge of a long, sweeping shoreline. It is wooded and spacious with a nice beach and an expansive view of the arm to the north and the main body of Yellowstone Lake beyond.

On day three you soon enter the hand-propelled zone of the lake. Your third camp, at Chipmunk Creek Outlet (5L3), is only 5 miles away, a short day of paddling. There is plenty of time to explore the shoreline, fish, watch birds, or go hiking once you get to camp. Much of the shoreline immediately south of camp was burned by the fires of 1988 and remains very open, but look for the recovery and growth of new trees taking place.

There are also other small bays and inlets that are fun to explore more closely.

Approaching the campsite at Plover Point.

Keep your eyes open for ospreys perching in dead trees along the shore or gliding over the water as they search for fish. Look, too, for pelicans and bald eagles all along this section of the paddle. Pelicans are common throughout the entire lake area, but bald eagles may be especially concentrated in this area at times. It is not unusual to see both adult and immature eagles as you approach the more wooded shoreline to the west and south of the marker designating the no-motor portion of the lake. Notice a small bay back to the west; look closely in this area for eagles, and if you see some, give them plenty of room, viewing from a distance. Do not paddle close enough to interfere with their activity or to make them take flight. This is a good place and time to use binoculars and a telephoto lens.

The end of the South Arm can be exceedingly calm at times, especially in the morning hours, since it is somewhat protected by the surrounding hillsides and mountains. South of the park lies the Thorofare region, deep within which the wild Upper Yellowstone River moves through meadows with the 10,115-foot-high Two Ocean Plateau rising to the west, and the steep towering cliffs of the northern Trident to the east. These mountains give you a good sense of the wildness that surrounds you.

You may want to paddle out to Peale Island, named after Albert Peale, mineralogist and medical doctor on the famous 1871 Hayden Expedition into Yellowstone. Off to the east, this island is home to another campsite and also a ranger cabin. At this point you are about 1 mile from Chipmunk Creek Outlet and your camp. This camp is set among trees and open meadows coming down to the shoreline. You'll probably arrive early at this camp, so settle in and enjoy the remoteness and wildness of the South Arm.

On day four, paddle back up to the northwest edge of the South Arm, camping at Plover Point (7M4), a distance of 9.5 miles. You retrace the western shoreline of the South Arm, exploring the landscape from the opposite perspective. This is the recommended route, and the safest. The other way to get to camp is to head north along the east shore, but the narrowest crossing available, heading west from just north of the no-motor marker, is a full mile.

A word to the wise: From here northward, the crossings get longer and riskier. A mile crossing may not appear to be much, especially in calm conditions, but if the winds pick up, a mile may become quite hazardous. Use caution and assess the risks based on your experience in the craft you are paddling. It is always better to stay near shore.

The camp at Plover Point is a dock site with the same boating and camping policies as Eagle Bay, your first night site. While this site does not offer the seclusion and privacy of others where you have been, it is a wonderful, very large beach site, and on a long, sandy point that gives you a far-reaching view down the South Arm and across the entire Yellowstone Lake from the east to the northwest. When you stay at this site you can really grasp the vastness of this lake wilderness. The beaches are great for exploring and there typically are nesting ospreys in the area. There is a small pond immediately behind the site where waterfowl can often be found, too.

The last day of paddling is a long one at 15 miles, and the last 5 miles across West Thumb are more than likely to be hard paddling into stiff headwinds. Leave early. The smaller bays along the way—Wolf and Breeze—may also prove harder to paddle than on your outbound trip. Take your time, pacing yourself for the miles remaining.

16 Sedge Bay to Brimstone Bay

Character: This trip is a simple paddle of the east shore of Yellowstone Lake for those seeking a *See map on pages 50–51* straightforward introduction to a backcountry paddling experience. The route travels along beaches, wooded shorelines, and rocky outcrops. There is also some hiking possible from camp.

Total paddling distance: 25 miles.

Suggested time: 2 days.

Put-in and take-out: Sedge Bay boat launch.

Difficulty: Moderate.

Campsites: Park Point North 5E9, Brimstone Bay 5E4.

Be aware of: Afternoon winds and accompanying waves, precautions for food storage in bear country.

Attractions: Remote paddling, bird watching (especially waterfowl), fishing.

Preparing to depart the Sedge Bay boat launch, with a view to the southwest across Yellowstone Lake.

Maps: USGS 7.5-minute Lake Butte–WY, Trail Lake–WY, Frank Island–WY.

Use: Light.

Directions: Sedge Bay is located at the northeast corner of Yellowstone Lake, just southeast of the more prominent Mary Bay. The Sedge Bay boat launch can be reached by driving approximately 8 miles east from Fishing Bridge to the last parking area before the road goes uphill and inland from the shoreline. Look for a pullout on the right between the road and the shore.

The paddling: Refer to trips 6 and 12 for more details about the route down the east shore of Yellowstone Lake. Try to depart by midmorning, even though you have a short day of paddling ahead, to avoid possible afternoon wind and the buildup of waves. Mornings are typically calmer than later in the day, and afternoon prevailing winds from the southeast can create rough water on this route.

The first night's camp, 6.25 miles down the shore, is Park Point North (5E9), an open site on a grassy hillside with a great panoramic view of the lake. Trip 9 describes this site in more detail. The Thorofare Trail is a short walk from camp, but bear management policies prohibit travel away from camp between April 1 and July 14.

The second day's destination is the campsite at Brimstone Bay (5E4). It is a large wooded site with a good take-out for boats. This location is in the 5-mile-per-hour zone of the lake, so any motor boats you may see will be moving very slowly. The Thorofare Trail passes near this site also and the same possible travel restriction applies here. As you are paddling from the north, you'll spot large, white, "snowlike" meadows on the wooded slopes to the east. These are the remnants of the extinct Brimstone Thermal Basin, and the camp is located below them, near the shore, about halfway along the wide bay.

As you paddle, look for a variety of birds along the shoreline and flying overhead. Ospreys can be seen perched in trees near the shore. Look for this large, whitish bird with a dark back. If in flight, the crooked long wings are conspicuous. If lucky, you may see this bird hover 100 feet or more above the water surface and suddenly fold its wings and plunge, hoping to catch a fish, its only food.

Bald eagles may also be nesting in the area. If you see either of these birds, please use care not to disturb them.

Pelicans are quite common, too, as they paddle in groups or fly overhead in formation. Along the shore, look for sandpipers scurrying along, probing the sand with their beaks for small insects.

Look, too, for seed-eating birds such as juncos and chickadees, flittering through the grass or the branches of conifers.

Day three is simply a return northward to Sedge Bay, a distance of 12.5 miles. Depending on your paddling speed, plan on from four to more than six hours to cover this shoreline distance. Large waves may slow you down further.

17 Sedge Bay to Southeast Arm

Character: This trip takes you way down into the Southeast Arm where you can see, and explore the remote interior of the park's water wilderness, including the mouth of the Yellowstone River. You will be able to wander through the wetland habitat at the south end and take a hike into wide-open meadows out of your second camp.

See map on pages 50–51

Total paddling distance: 42 miles.
Suggested time: 4 days
Put-in and take-out: Sedge Bay boat launch.
Difficulty: Moderate to difficult.
Campsites: Columbine Meadow North 5E6, Southeast Arm Inlet 6A2, Brimstone Bay 5E4.
Be aware of: Afternoon winds and accompanying waves, precautions for food storage in bear country.
Attractions: Remote paddling, bird watching (especially waterfowl), fishing, hiking.
Maps: USGS 7.5-minute Lake Butte–WY, Frank Island–WY, Sylvan Lake–WY, Trail Lake–WY, Alder Lake–WY.
Use: Light to moderate.
Directions: Sedge Bay is located at the northeast corner of Yellowstone Lake, just southeast of the more prominent Mary Bay. The Sedge Bay boat launch can be reached by driving approximately 8 miles east from Fishing Bridge to the last parking area before the

road goes uphill and inland from the shoreline. Look for a pullout on the right between the road and the shore.

The paddling: This trip includes two days of paddling more than 10 miles each day. Refer to trip descriptions 6, 12, and 16 for greater detail about the first 14 miles of the east shoreline and some things to expect along the way.

Your first night's destination is Columbine Meadow North (5E6), 10 miles down the shoreline. It is a very large camp, capable of holding up to 20 people and is accessible to both hikers and horsepack outfits using the Thorofare Trail. As with many sites around the lake, off-trail travel is prohibited between April 1 and July 14, an important time to minimize interference with bears feeding on spawning trout. The site is flat, wooded, and easily accessible from the water. It is located just north of the point on shore designating the start of the 5-mile-per-hour zone for motorboat operators. Visits to this site are limited to one night.

The second day follows a wooded, sometimes rocky, and sandy shoreline 11 miles to camp two, Southeast Arm Inlet (6A2). The route from your first night to this camp is a pleasant and interesting paddle, especially when you round the shoreline bend to the east and get views of the mountains to the south. Here you also get your first good look at the end of the arm and the mouth of the Yellowstone River. If you get a reasonably early start in the morning, you should have ample time to meander around the bays and inlets before heading to camp.

There are lots of waterfowl frequenting this area, including Canada geese,

Unsettled weather gathers over a typical beach along the east side of Yellowstone Lake.

mallard ducks, and the common merganser, the sleek, low-riding bird that, in flight, assumes a perfectly straight, horizontal position. The male has a white body with a black back, and a green-black head. The female, gray in color with a crested, rufous head, is often seen with her flock of young paddling along behind, or even catching a free ride on her back.

You may also spot gadwall, American wigeon, and pintail ducks in the spring and fall. Barrow's goldeneye, a nesting species in the park, is readily identified in the male by the white crescent in front of the eye. The female has a gray body, brown head, and a light collar. They lay their 6 to 12 green eggs in cavities in trees.

Paddle slowly and quietly through here, minimizing your disturbance to these waterfowl as much as possible, while enjoying the intimacy of the place. It is very hidden and protected.

As you approach this camp, do not be put off by its burned-over appearance. While it was burned in the 1988 fires, live trees remain and thousands of young lodgepole pines are coming back in.

Tent sites are limited here. Use caution around dead trees that could fall. The fire pit and cook area overlook the entire Southeast Arm. There is also a small bay on the west side of the camp, so you are actually staying on a short peninsula. A trail leads out of the site to a series of large meadows, but the trail is not obvious. Look for orange markers up the slope behind camp and through the woods. These guide you until the trail becomes clearer. This entire camp is closed from May 15

A storm is brewing over the Southeast Arm. At such times it makes great sense to paddle near the shore.

to July 14 to give bears in the area uninterrupted access to their food source— spawning trout.

On the third day, return eastward through the end of the arm and then northward along the shore to Brimstone Bay camp (5E4), 8.5 miles distant. This is your shortest day of paddling. Weather permitting, you can linger around camp and explore or fish as you head up to Brimstone Bay.

On the final day, head 12.5 miles straight back to Sedge Bay.

A word to the wise: Plan on at least four to six hours to complete this paddle. Chances are good that afternoon wind buildup and large waves will slow your progress.

18 Sedge Bay to Trail Bay

Character: This is an easy-paced trip down the east shore of Yellowstone Lake to Trail Bay at the very southeast corner of the South Arm, near the inlet of the Yellowstone River. There is ample time to paddle the bays and inlets of the arm, with perhaps even a hike included.

See map on pages 50–51

Total paddling distance: 36 miles.

Suggested time: 4 days.

Put-in and take-out: Sedge Bay boat launch.

Difficulty: Moderate to difficult.

Campsites: Park Point South 5E8, Trail Bay 6A4, Columbine Meadow North 5E6.

Be aware of: Afternoon winds and accompanying waves, precautions for food storage in bear country.

Attractions: Bird watching (especially waterfowl), fishing, hiking.

Maps: USGS 7.5-minute Lake Butte–WY, Frank Island–WY, Sylvan Lake–WY, Trail Lake–WY, Alder Lake–WY.

Use: Light to moderate.

Directions: Sedge Bay is located at the northeast corner of Yellowstone Lake, just southeast of the more prominent Mary Bay. The Sedge Bay boat launch can be reached by driving approximately 8 miles east from Fishing Bridge to the last parking area before the road goes uphill and inland from the shoreline. Look for a pullout on the right between the road and the shore.

The paddling: This trip is perfect for those wanting a true backcountry experience with easy to moderate paddling each day. Review descriptions for trips 6, 12, 16, and 17 for more information about traveling the east shore. The first night's destination for this trip, the Park Point South site (5E8), is 7 miles down the shore. It is a large, flat site with a long beach and wide-open view of the lake, with Frank Island directly west. Meadow Creek enters the lake just north of the camp. If you bushwhack a couple of hundred yards through the woods behind camp, you'll come to the Thorofare Trail and a large meadow. This is a nice side trip from camp, but travel away from camp is not allowed between April 1 and July 14 to lessen encounters with bears.

On day two, you paddle 11 miles farther south to the far end of the Southeast Arm and Trail Bay camp (6A4), located on the south side of the bay, near the inlet of Trail Creek. To get to this camp, you enter the no-motor zone and paddle along the shallow wetland where the Yellowstone River enters the lake. There are many small bays and channels to wander into either on your way to camp or after you've set up.

Spawning activity in the many small streams around Yellowstone Lake is quite a spectacle—the waters become virtually clogged with trout moving to their spawning beds. Males arrive first and await the arrival of the females. The female, often fighting with other females for the best site, chooses a nest in the gravel of the streambed where she digs out a cavity about 6 inches deep. The rapid sideways fanning of her tail creates the dishlike depression. She is joined by the male, and, in synch, she releases eggs while he releases sperm into the nest cavity. The eggs are then covered with gravel by the female. An average 14-inch female carries about 1,000 eggs.

Competition between males can take place throughout the spawning act. Often a male will leave the nest to chase off other fish just as the female releases her eggs. Eggs that may drift downstream are eaten by other males and by gulls that gather to partake in the feast. Grizzly bears gather along these streams to join the fish buffet, along with foraging pelicans.

The Park Point South campsite is on a hillside above the Southeast Arm.

Because Trail Bay camp is so near important spawning habitat, it is closed from May 15 to July 14 to give bears in the area uninterrupted access to their food source.

If you are up for an easy hike, Trail Creek Trail is just behind camp and Trail Lake can be reached in about 2 to 2.5 miles by hiking east through some marshy terrain to the turnoff up to the lake.

The third day is a northward paddle, retracing your route 8 miles to Columbine Meadow North (5E6). See trip 17 for details about this camp. On the last day, your fourth, you have a straightforward 10-mile paddle back to Sedge Bay.

19 Sedge Bay to Southeast Arm

Character: This trip is one day longer than trip 17, but essentially the same. It includes a day to layover at the Southeast Arm Inlet camp with an optional day hike. Don't forget your hiking boots.

See map on pages 50–51

Total paddling distance: 42 miles.

Suggested time: 5 days.

Put-in and take-out: Sedge Bay boat launch.

Difficulty: Moderate to difficult.

Suggested campsites: Brimstone Point 5E3, Southeast Arm Inlet 6A2, Brimstone Bay 5E4.

Be aware of: Afternoon winds and accompanying waves, precautions for food storage in bear country.

Attractions: Bird watching (especially waterfowl), fishing, day hiking.

Maps: USGS 7.5-minute Lake Butte–WY, Frank Island–WY, Sylvan Lake–WY, Trail Lake–WY, Alder Lake–WY.

Use: Light to moderate.

Directions: Sedge Bay is located at the northeast corner of Yellowstone Lake, just southeast of the more prominent Mary Bay. The Sedge Bay boat launch can be reached by driving approximately 8 miles east from Fishing Bridge to the last parking area before the road goes uphill and inland from the shoreline. Look for a pullout on the right between the road and the shore.

The paddling: Read the description for trip 17 carefully to give you details for this trip. The route, total distance, and destination camp are identical for this trip. The difference is the number of miles paddled each day and two different camps where you stay.

The first day follows the shoreline 14 miles to Brimstone Point (5E3), a site almost hidden in the woods, but near shore. This site has the restriction that prohibits travel away from camp from April 1 to July 14.

Day two is just 7 miles around the lower end of the arm to the camp at Southeast Arm Inlet (6A2). As described in trip 17, this end of the arm is worth exploring and you have plenty of time on this day to do that.

Always keep a sharp eye for pelicans, bald eagles, and ospreys, all of which rely exclusively on the native Yellowstone cutthroat trout for food. Keep a cautious distance from them so as not to disturb them. Frightening them into flight wastes their energy.

Common mergansers, the low-riding, slender fish-eating duck, dive for their food and will also dive if you approach too closely. The male has a beautiful dark green head, while the female's is rust-colored and crested. When flying, they move very quickly, close to the water's surface, with their body straight and horizontal. Other ducks in flight show a more pronounced curve between head and neck.

Another duck frequently seen in the area is the common goldeneye, recognized by its dark back and head, with a white breast and conspicuous white spot in front of the eye. In flight, the male flashes large, white squares on its wings, and a whistling sound can be heard with the rapid beating of his wings.

The third day is the day to layover. The optional hike out of this camp is a remote backcountry experience through forest, meadows, and wetlands. To find the trail, look for an orange trail marker up the slope from camp. Walk to it and with some careful looking, you'll see other markers that will guide you. There is a lot of downfall and some boggy areas. Just keep following the markers; some can be hard to find but before long the trail becomes more distinct.

Stay on the trail to avoid harming the fragile wetlands and meadows. The boggy areas are usually small, shallow bodies of water that have filled slowly over the years with organic material and are dominated by mosses and sedges as

A campfire on the shore of the Southeast Arm.

succession to other wetland habitats progresses. Sedges are grasslike plants, while mosses grow in dense mats. These areas are often referred to as peat bogs since the decomposed plant material is called peat. Depending on the amount of water in the basin, numerous aquatic invertebrates will be found here, which become food for fish, amphibians, and birds.

Meadows come in two forms in the arid West: sedge-meadows and sedge-grass-meadows. Sedge-meadows are dominated by sedges on top of firm sod and are often covered by a few inches of water during the spring growing season. Sedge-grass-meadows are located on drier, more elevated sites.

One last wetland area to consider is the shrub-swamp community. Here, where the water table remains near the surface, willows dominate.

Each of these areas are important ecologically because they are so rich in verte-brate species.

Within 0.5 mile of camp, along a very small creek, you will come to a marked trail junction showing distances to various points. From the trail junction, you can go east around the end of the Southeast Arm, or go west about 1 mile to another junction. If you go west, look for a large marker on a post in the middle of a meadow. From the marker, you can head south along Chipmunk Creek or farther west toward the South Arm of Yellowstone Lake. You are in the lower reaches of the park here, about 12 miles from its southern border.

If you choose to head west you are only about 1.5 miles from the South Arm, an easy round-trip hike. In about 1 mile you come to a creek that leads to a large inlet at the east side of the arm. There is no trail going along the creek to the lake, but it is open country and quite easy to find your way.

When you are ready to return to camp, use care to retrace your steps, looking for markers and landmarks spotted on the way in.

20 Sedge Bay to Promontory Southeast

Character: While this trip starts off easily with a very short day, the remaining four days each

See map on pages 50–51

contain more than 10 miles of paddling. It's a good choice if you must have a late start the first day but you want to see a lot of the Southeast Arm and are in condition for long paddles.

Total paddling distance: 52 miles.

Suggested time: 5 days.

Put-in and take-out: Sedge Bay boat launch.

Difficulty: Moderate to difficult.

Suggested campsites: Midshore 5H1, Brimstone Point 5E3, Promontory Southeast 6A1, Brimstone Bay 5E4.

Be aware of: Afternoon winds and accompanying waves, precautions for food storage in bear country.

Attractions: Remote paddling, bird watching (especially waterfowl), fishing.

Maps: USGS 7.5-minute Lake Butte–WY, Frank Island–WY, Sylvan Lake–WY, Trail Lake–WY, Alder Lake–WY.

Use: Light to moderate.

Directions: Sedge Bay is located at the northeast corner of Yellowstone Lake, just southeast of the more prominent Mary Bay. The Sedge Bay boat launch can be reached by driving approximately 8 miles east from Fishing Bridge to the last parking area before the road goes uphill and inland from the shoreline. Look for a pullout on the right between the road and the shore.

The paddling: This trip covers more of the shoreline than any of the previously described trips out of Sedge Bay. From Sedge, it takes you down the east shore and around the Southeast Arm to that body's west side. Review trips 6, 12, 17, 18, and 19 for additional details about the route. The first day is a very short one, paddling just 3.75 miles to the Midshore campsite (5H1), a small, two-tent site limited to six people. This site is wooded, flat, and open enough to be sunny. It has a great view of the lake, as do all the sites along this shore, and a long, gravel beach immediately adjacent. This site is closed April 1 to August 10 each year to reduce conflicts between humans and bears.

The second day of paddling takes you 10.25 miles farther down the shore to Brimstone Point camp (5E3), a heavily wooded site about halfway into the Southeast Arm. There is no travel away from camp between April 1 and July 14, but after that time you may want to explore behind camp and hike some of the

A storm has dumped hail on a beach along Yellowstone Lake.

Thorofare Trail that parallels the entire east shore of the lake.

The destination on day three is Promontory Southeast (6A1), a campsite tucked in a small bay, with a large meadow coming down to the beach immediately adjacent to the site. The paddle to this site takes you around the entire end of the arm, 12 miles from your last camp. If you feel you have time and the energy to explore some, be sure to check out the calm areas hidden in the willows along the shore, especially where the Yellowstone River enters the lake. There are usually lots of waterfowl here. Keep alert and try not to disturb them.

Moose are not common here, but there are occasional sightings. If you are really lucky, you may even see a moose cow with her calf. The calf is born in late May or June. It has the characteristic bell, a wattle-like flap of skin hanging below the chin, but no back hump, and the legs are even longer, proportionally, than the mother's. Unlike young deer and elk, the young moose is not spotted, but a uniform bay color. After a few weeks near the birthplace, the calf begins to travel with the cow. They are inseparable for about a year, or until the process begins again with the cow preparing to give birth once more.

As elsewhere on Yellowstone Lake, keep alert to bald eagles soaring overhead or perched in shoreline trees, where they keep an "eagle eye" on possible fish meals. In the summer of 1997, I saw five fledging bald eagles in one tree in this area. You may see either eagles or ospreys, the fish hawks with the crooked wings, carrying fish, always head first, in their talons back to their young in the nest. Occasionally the heads of the young birds can be seen poking above the edge of the nest. Keep your binoculars or telephoto lens handy and always keep far enough away to cause no disturbance to the birds.

On the fourth day you begin your return trip by paddling 13.5 miles to Brimstone Bay camp (5E4), just north of your second night camp. It is a large site, with the common April 1 through July 14 travel restriction. While sitting around camp on your last night, walk down to the beach and you'll get a view of much of what you have paddled the last few days. Sunsets on this beach are often beautiful.

Day five, your last on Yellowstone Lake, concludes with a final 12.5 mile trip up the shore to Sedge Bay. You have paddled quite a few miles, but believe it or not, the 26 miles to your farthest camp is not even a fourth of the lake's total shoreline. This is a big lake and there are many more wilderness trips awaiting your return.

7. Paddling Trips in Grand Teton National Park

Jackson Lake and four nearby smaller lakes, Leigh, String, Jenny, and Two Ocean, offer a range of paddling experiences for canoe and touring kayaks in one of the most beautiful mountain settings in the country. All but Leigh Lake are easily accessed by vehicle.

Park Service policy permits motorized boats on Jackson and Jenny lakes. Motor boats, jet skis, sail boats, and sail boards are allowed on Jackson Lake, but because of its large size, conflicts with hand-propelled craft can be minimized or are nonexistent. Motorized boats are also permitted on Jenny Lake, but there is an 8-horsepower limit.

Jackson Lake is a large lake nearly 17 miles long and 9 miles wide, with about 70 miles of shoreline. Numerous bays, inlets, islands, and open water are available for exploring on day trips or more extended excursions. There are fifteen campsites accessible by water, with five located on islands. All sites have wonderful views of the dramatic mountain and lake landscape.

Wildlife abounds in the region, so keep a lookout on the water and along the shore. Bird life and various mammals, large and small, can also be seen. Keep your eyes open for moose, elk, and a diversity of waterfowl, sometimes with family in tow. Bears are not uncommon, and have occasionally been seen swimming to Elk Island, or even across the lake north of Colter Bay!

Floating the Snake River can add greatly to your paddling adventures, and offer a change of pace from lake cruising. Originating in the mountains near the southern end of Yellowstone Park, this river has many moods as it flows toward Grand Teton National Park and eventually through 27 miles of diverse current within the park. Keep in mind that while the river does wind its way through meanders and braided channels, it can be quite powerful, cold, and swift along certain stretches and at any time of the year, and especially during the spring snow melt. I don't recommend that inexperienced paddlers attempt this river, except perhaps in the slower moving current of the Oxbow Bend area just downstream from the Jackson Lake dam. This river habitat is rich and diverse, so keep your eyes open for wildlife and bird life along the bank and in the water.

Grand Teton National Park

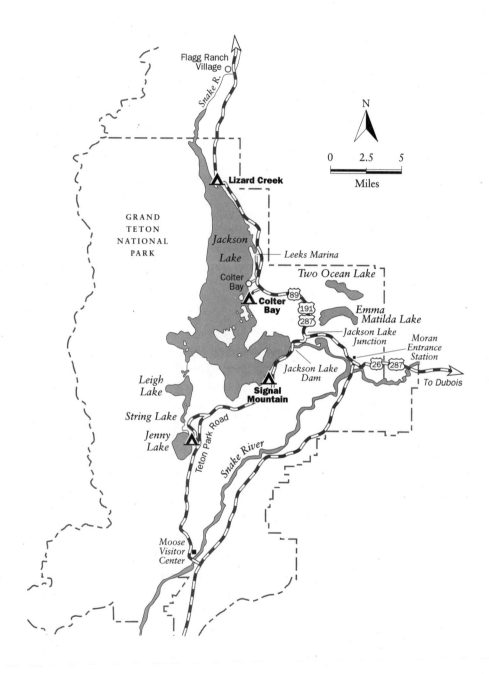

Flagg Ranch
Village

Snake R.

N

0   2.5   5

Miles

⛺ **Lizard Creek**

GRAND
TETON
NATIONAL
PARK

*Jackson
Lake*

Colter
Bay

⛺ **Colter
Bay**

Leeks Marina

Two Ocean Lake

89

191

287

*Emma
Matilda Lake*

*Jackson Lake
Junction*

Moran
Entrance
Station

26 287

*Jackson Lake
Dam*

⛺
**Signal
Mountain**

*Leigh
Lake*

To Dubois

String Lake

*Jenny
Lake*

⛺

Teton Park Road

Snake River

Moose
Visitor
Center

Day trips

There are many day-paddling possibilities throughout Grand Teton National Park. Jenny, String, Leigh, and Jackson lakes are located adjacent to each other at the base of the Teton Range and are easily accessible by vehicle. Two Ocean Lake, a short distance to the east of Jackson Lake, is also a wonderfully secluded place to paddle and easily reached for launching your canoe or kayak. The Snake River also has some exciting paddling, including some novice to intermediate trips briefly described here.

21 String Lake

Character: A peaceful, short paddle on a small, shallow lake that sits directly below the Tetons; excellent for beginners.

See map on page 104

Total paddling distance: About 3 miles.
Average paddling time: 1–2 hours.
Put-in and take-out: String Lake Trailhead.
Difficulty: Easy.
Be aware of: Wind and accompanying waves, even on smaller lakes.
Attractions: Beautiful mountain backdrop adjacent to the lake, clear water, swimming, bird life. Bring a camera.
Map: USGS 7.5-minute Jenny Lake–WY.
Use: Moderate to heavy.
Directions: The parking lot for the String Lake Trailhead is located by turning west off Teton Park Road at North Jenny Lake Junction. Follow the signs to Jenny Lake Lodge and String Lake, about 3 miles down the road. Just before the lodge, the road to the boat launch turns right, dead-ending at String Lake.

The paddling: String Lake is perfect for a short, easy paddle. Situated at the base of the Teton Range, it is one of the most beautiful places you will ever paddle. It is a great place for families, too, since the water is quite shallow (10 feet at its deepest) and relatively warm compared to other lakes in the area.

The boat launch and parking area are about halfway along the east shoreline. Remember that only self-propelled boats are permitted here. The parking area can get quite crowded, so plan to arrive early in the day. There is a 3.5-mile trail around the lake, too, if you or some of your party would like to do some hiking.

String Lake, surrounded by lodgepole pine, spruce, and fir trees, is about 1 mile long and, except for the south end that widens to about 0.25 mile, quite narrow, making it feel a bit like a river. String is really a connection between Jenny Lake to the south and Leigh Lake to the north. The paddle to the north end of the lake takes you to the Leigh Lake outlet.

String Lake is also used by paddlers going on to Leigh Lake for day or overnight trips. There is a short portage on the east bank near the north end of the lake.

Leigh Lake, String Lake, and Jenny Lake

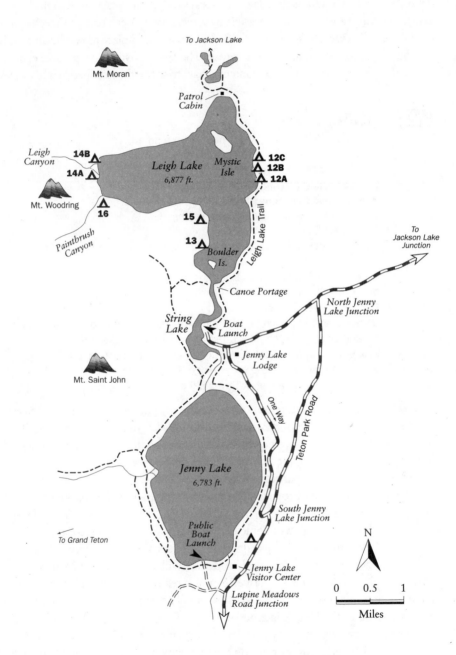

A walkway leads to the boat launch and trailhead at String Lake.

22 Jenny Lake

Character: A beautiful, small lake in the shadow of the Tetons. Bring your camera and fishing gear.

Total paddling distance: About 5 miles.

Average paddling time: 2–3 hours.

Put-in and take-out: Jenny Lake boat launch (at south end of lake)

Difficulty: Easy to moderate.

Be aware of: Winds and waves, sometimes strong and developing quickly. Prevailing southwest winds can funnel through Cascade Canyon.

Attractions: Rocky shoreline and bottom, bird watching, hiking, fishing.

Maps: USGS 7.5-minute Jenny Lake–WY, Moose–WY.

Use: Light to moderate.

Directions: The public boat launch on Jenny Lake is a small, simple affair at the very south end of the lake. There are no signs guiding you to this point, but it is easily located. Turn west on Lupine Meadows Road at its junction with Teton Park Road. (This junction is just south of the Jenny Lake Visitor Center and Jenny Lake Trailhead.) After crossing the bridge over the creek, turn right on the dirt road and drive the few hundred yards north to its end at the lake, bearing left as you go. There is a small gravel boat launch and a parking area. Don't be confused by the signs to the East Shore Boat Dock, the landing for a shuttle boat.

Taking a rest on the north shore of Jenny Lake, with Cascade Canyon in the background.

The paddling: The setting is breathtaking. The lake is lined with shrubs and a spruce-fir forest, with the Tetons thrusting skyward thousands of feet just to your left, along the west shore of the lake. The water, as is in almost all the lakes in the area, is crystal clear with a rocky bottom.

Most of the lakes in this area, including Jenny Lake, were created by the gouging and scouring of glaciers tens of thousands of years ago. The first part of this 5-mile clockwise paddle of Jenny Lake's shoreline takes you along the base of the mountains to the mouth of Cascade Canyon, the best example of the glaciated valley found throughout this range. A mass of ice more than 1,000 feet thick once flowed down this canyon, eventually pushing its pile of debris across from where you are now paddling and coming to a rest just to the east, where it left the high rim of land that forms the east shore of the lake.

You will no doubt see the park concessionaire's shuttle boat ferrying people back and forth from Cascade Canyon to the East Shore Boat Dock. People not wanting to walk the entire shoreline of the lake use this shuttle to get to and from the Cascade Canyon Trailhead. Motor boats are permitted on Jenny Lake, but motors are restricted to 8 horsepower.

You can land at the trailhead and walk the 0.5 mile to Hidden Falls, and past Inspiration Point before heading as far into the canyon as you have time for. This is a highly recommended hike.

On the very north edge of the lake as you continue paddling, you come to the inlet of the creek from String Lake just to the north. Fly fishers are often seen angling for trout at this air-enriched part of the lake. This lake has populations of the native Snake River cutthroat trout and mackinaw, or lake trout. Lake trout, although not native to the region, thrive in deep lakes such as Jenny, where depths reach 236 feet. These fish prefer a water temperature between 38 to 55 degrees. They also travel near lake bottoms because oxygen levels there are high due to minimal decay of plant life.

Lake trout spawn in the fall. According to some experts, this timing often coincides with the first ice formation along the lakeshores. It is believed that the ice may serve to protect these deep-water fish from predators when they are in the more shallow waters spawning.

Due to the cold water temperatures, lake trout here grow more slowly and do not grow as large as in other areas in North America. Even so, these trout can reach 10 to 20 pounds and on occasion, 30 or more pounds.

As you paddle along the north end of the lake, there are several narrow gravel beaches where you can stop and rest.

Jenny Lake, by the way, was named after the Shoshone Indian wife of nineteenth-century local explorer and trapper, Beaver Dick Leigh. His wife, Jenny, and their six children died of smallpox during the winter of 1876. The beauty of this lake is a fitting tribute.

After you begin to head south along the east shore of the lake, you will notice cars on the road paralleling the shore, 75 yards above the water. This is the one-

The public boat launch at the south end of Jenny Lake.

way road coming south from the Jenny Lake Lodge and String Lake area. It meets the Teton Park Road just north of the southern Jenny Lake development with its campground, ranger station, store, climbing school, and boat shuttle.

A relaxed paddle of this lake will take about 2 to 3 hours, longer if you opt to take a hike.

23 String Lake to Leigh Lake

Character: This trip goes north through String Lake, over a short portage, to Leigh Lake, a beautiful, remote lake with two islands and great views of the Tetons immediately to the west.

> See map on page 104

Total paddling distance: Approximately 7 miles (plus a portage of approximately 100 yards).
Average paddling time: 4–6 hours.
Put-in and take-out: String Lake boat launch.
Difficulty: Easy to moderate.
Be aware of: Wind and waves on Leigh Lake, especially in the west arm that leads to Leigh and Paintbrush canyons.
Attractions: Calm, riverlike paddle on the north end of String Lake, the beautiful mountain lake setting of Leigh Lake, great views of the Tetons, fishing, bird watching.
Maps: USGS 7.5-minute Jenny Lake–WY, Mt. Moran–WY.
Use: Easy to moderate.
Directions: The parking lot for the String Lake Trailhead is located by turning west off Teton Park Road at North Jenny Lake Junction. Follow the signs to Jenny Lake Lodge and String Lake, about 3 miles down the road. Just before the lodge, the road to the boat launch bears right, dead-ending at String Lake.

The paddling: This trip includes the only portage, as brief as it is, in this entire guide. See the description for trip 21 which gives details for String Lake. The destination for this trip is Leigh Lake, so head directly north on String Lake, through this calm, almost riverlike section. The portage is about 1.25 miles away, or 10 to 15 minutes. Look for the portage in the trees along the east shore as the lake narrows. Make room for others as you move in to shore. Congestion can occur here during busier times, so make your portage as efficient as possible, allowing people faster than you to move by.

The portage is a short, slightly uphill 5- to 10-minute walk on a wide trail. As you approach Leigh Lake, the trail becomes a set of wide log steps dropping about 20 feet to a small, sandy beach at the water's edge. Watch your footing on these steps. Their slope is steep and especially noticeable when you are carrying a boat. The portage ends at the south end of Leigh Lake.

This is another beautifully carved glacial lake, with dramatic views of the Tetons towering on the west side, and Leigh and Paintbrush canyons sweeping out of them into the west arm of the lake. It was named for Beaver Dick Leigh, a

The portage steps from String Lake to Leigh Lake.

nineteenth-century local mountain man and trapper who guided the Ferdinand Hayden expedition through the Jackson Hole area during the 1870s.

Leigh Lake is about 2 miles long, north to south, with a 7-mile shoreline. This trip follows the shoreline counterclockwise. As you paddle the shoreline you will see hints of the eight campsites scattered along the way. A trail follows the east shoreline on its way to Bearpaw Lake, north of Leigh Lake, and can make for a nice side hike if you have time. If you are so inclined, beach your boat at the northeast side of the lake and pick up the trail in the woods. Head west and look for signs indicating the way to Bearpaw Lake. Trapper Lake is just to the north, and an unnamed one to the east. Parties have portaged through this area to Bearpaw Bay on Jackson Lake. Keep a sharp lookout for moose all along this north shore.

While the wooded east shore is quite flat, the surrounding landscape becomes increasingly steep as you head west. The glacier on the south side of Mount Moran, the large peak immediately to the northwest, has been known to drop icebergs into Leigh Lake in midsummer. This last occurred in the mid-1980s.

Mystic Isle, the large island at the north end of the lake, is off-limits to visitors because of nesting eagles, but you can paddle around it. Pause long enough to take a good look at the Teton Range directly ahead of you. This is a beautiful, calendar-perfect setting with high, snow-covered peaks, and two steep canyons coming out of them, ending at the lake.

The remaining paddle takes you around the west side of the lake, eventually returning to the portage. You know you are almost there when you spot Boulder Island, just north of the portage.

24 Two Ocean Lake

Character: This small lake, set in the moraines left by the glaciers that formed Pacific Creek, is somewhat off the beaten path, just east of the Jackson Lake area. It is a wonderful place to paddle if you are looking for a quiet, calm experience with opportunities to fish, watch birds, and maybe spot a moose.

See map on page 112

Total paddling distance: 6 miles.

Average paddling time: 2–3 hours.

Put-in and take-out: Parking lot at Two Ocean Lake Trailhead and picnic area.

Difficulty: Easy.

Be aware of: Afternoon winds and storm buildup, bear country precautions.

Attractions: Abundant wildflowers and bird life; fishing, hiking; sign of beaver, elk, and moose.

Map: USGS 7.5-minute Two Ocean Lake–WY.

Use: Light.

Directions: Two Ocean Lake can be reached by turning north on Pacific Creek Road, 1 mile west of the Moran Entrance. Drive 2 miles on this paved road along Pacific Creek to the signed junction; turn left to the lake. This narrow, dirt road can be rutted and rough, and slick in wet weather, but it is a beautiful 2.5-mile drive through forests of aspen and fir. The road is sometimes closed during rainy periods, so check at a ranger station for road conditions.

The paddling: This is a wonderful, 2.5-mile long, glacially carved lake in a serene setting. Surrounded by conifer forests and meadows of wildflowers, the quiet shoreline is perfect for a leisurely half-day exploration.

After unloading boat and gear at the parking area, you have to carry it down a short path to the lake shore. There is no formal boat launch, but the path to the put-in is obvious; it begins just past the trail sign. This is the kind of lake to just mosey around, looking for bird life, signs of beaver, and the occasional elk or moose. Bring binoculars and a bird book, too. The wildflowers can be especially abundant in late June and well into July, and a wildflower guide can be fun to have along.

The almost mythical image of the beaver, the great flat-tailed, mountain fur-bearer that drove international economies and brought countries to war, surrounds you here, as do the ghosts of mountain men who wandered these mountains 150 years ago in search of this valuable mammal, setting their traps in these lakes.

The fur of this, the largest North American rodent, motivated exploration and eventual conquest of the continent. The search for beaver fur brought the French

Two Ocean Lake

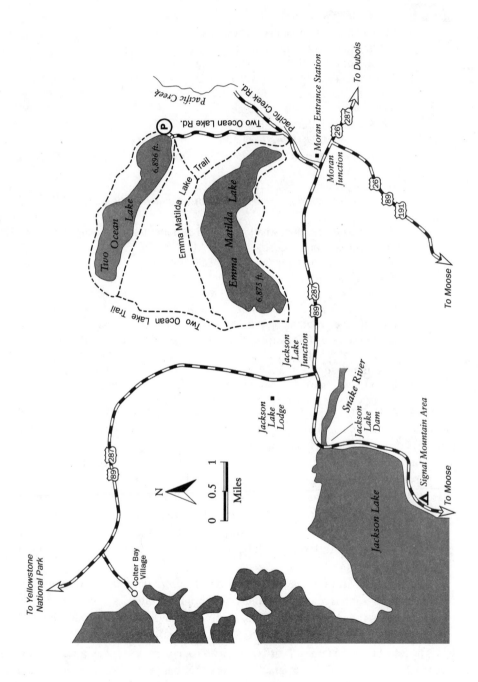

to the eastern shores of North America in the early seventeenth century. Trade with Indians brought the natives into the Iron Age. Striving for a monopoly in the fur trade, the French had little tolerance for the British, who wanted to share the treasures of the beaver. Many small military engagements occured between the British, French, and Indians, as did intertribal conflicts. Bitterness grew, culminating in the French and Indian War midway through the eighteenth century. After seven years of war, France lost its 200-year dominance of the beaver trade to the British Empire.

An elusive rodent, the beaver paddles with its large, webbed feet, using its flat, hairless tail as a rudder, through quiet waters in search of willows, aspen, cottonwood, and other aquatic plants. These trees and plants serve as both food and building materials for the animal's lodges and dams. You may be lucky enough to spot one as you paddle your way through these waters.

More likely, though, is the opportunity to see signs of beaver. Look for small, muddy trails leading out of the water or the characteristic stick-covered, dome-shaped lodge. This sometimes massive, exceedingly strong structure, with its underwater entrance, is built in water deep enough not to freeze and is home to the beaver family throughout the year. The young, generally numbering four or so, are born in the lodge, where the severe winters are kept at bay by the thick mud walls. The beaver can exit the lodge, swim under the thick ice surface, and bring back food it has stored on the lake bottom the previous fall.

Beavers build dams, when necessary, to create ponds in streams or to increase the depths of shallow ponds. The pond is a refuge from enemies, a place to cache food, and like the lodge, has to be deep enough to prevent full freezing. Beaver have an important ecological influence in an area, often transforming a simple stream valley into a place of ponds and lakes where new aquatic plants can take hold, and fish and waterfowl find food and shelter. In time, however, the beaver's food sources usually dwindle and it moves on, leaving a changed landscape.

Among the good trails in this area, Two Ocean Lake Trail follows the north shore of the lake before bending to the south and ascending 1 mile to Grand View Point (7,586 feet), with spectacular views of the Teton Range and Jackson Lake. A branch at the eastern end of the lake leads southwest to the Emma Matilda Lake Trail. Trails in the area, due to heavy vegetation and light use, are sometimes indistinct. Keep alert to where you are hiking. Remember that a boat permit is required for this lake, as for all lakes in Grand Teton Park.

JACKSON LAKE

25 Signal Mountain to Donoho Point and Hermitage Point

Overview: This day trip tours part of the southeast portion of Jackson Lake as you paddle north around Donoho Point, an island.

See map on page 115

Total paddling distance: 6–8 miles.
Average paddling time: 3–4 hours.
Put-in and take-out: Signal Mountain boat launch.
Difficulty: Easy to moderate.
Be aware of: Afternoon winds and accompanying waves.
Attractions: Open-water paddling, incredible views of the Teton Range, bird watching (especially water birds), fishing, hiking.
Maps: USGS 7.5-minute Moran–WY, Jenny Lake–WY.
Use: Light.
Directions: The turnoff for the Signal Mountain launch is located along Teton Park Road on the southeast shore of Jackson Lake, 3 miles south of Jackson Lake Junction and approximately 9 miles north of the Jenny Lake area. After turning west off the main road, follow the signs through the lodge area and development down to the large parking area and boat launch.

The paddling: Jackson Lake is a long, large lake backed up against the Teton Range. With a convoluted shoreline of approximately 70 miles and islands scattered throughout its southern end, Jackson offers many paddling opportunities of

Paddling toward Hermitage Point from Donoho Point, with Mount Moran in the background.

South Jackson Lake

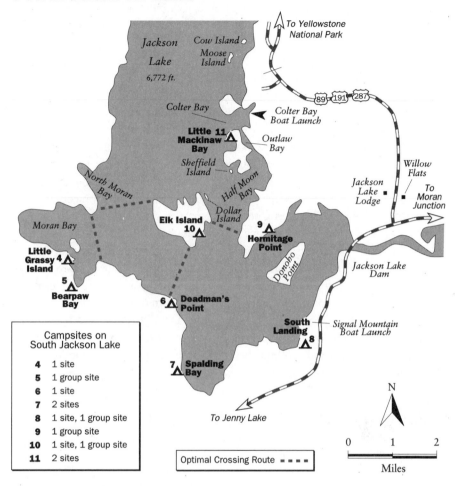

Jackson
Lake
6,772 ft.

Cow Island
Moose
Island

To Yellowstone
National Park

89 191 287

Colter Bay

Colter Bay
Boat Launch

**Little 11
Mackinaw
Bay**

Outlaw
Bay

Sheffield
Island

Willow
Flats

Jackson
Lake
Lodge

To
Moran
Junction

North Moran Bay

Half Moon Bay

**Elk Island
10**

Dollar
Island

**9
Hermitage
Point**

Moran Bay

Donoho
Point

Jackson Lake
Dam

**Little
Grassy 4
Island**

**5
Bearpaw
Bay**

**6 Deadman's
Point**

South
Landing

8

Signal Mountain
Boat Launch

Campsites on South Jackson Lake	
4	1 site
5	1 group site
6	1 site
7	2 sites
8	1 site, 1 group site
9	1 group site
10	1 site, 1 group site
11	2 sites

**7 Spalding
Bay**

To Jenny Lake

Optimal Crossing Route ■ ■ ■ ■

N

0   1   2
Miles

varying lengths. This day trip provides an introduction to the lake with a 6-to-8-mile route through part of its southeast section. Bring along binoculars and a bird book, too, because there will be water birds on the lake and shoreline paddling will be close enough to do some spotting from your boat. Fishing can also be good.

Starting at the Signal Mountain boat launch, head to Donoho Point, the island about 0.5 mile to the northwest. Mornings are typically calm and the views of the Teton Range from here, often reflected in the lake, are astounding. As you approach the island, paddle north along the shore. You are looking toward the Willow Flats area with Jackson Lake Lodge on the hillside. This is one of three lodges in Grand Teton National Park, and it's large enough to accommodate large conferences, along with having a spectacular view across Jackson Lake to the Teton skyline. Most of the 385 guest rooms are in cottages surrounding the main lodge,

115

where meals are served. The main lodge houses an assortment of Native American artifacts and Western art, as well as a gift and apparel shop.

Jackson Lake Dam is off to the east. Yes, this lake does have a dam, and while controversial at times, it was built before this area was added to the national park system in 1950. Originally built of logs in 1906 to provide irrigation water for Idaho farmers and flood control for residents of Jackson Hole, it was washed out in 1914. A concrete dam was completed on the site in 1916.

As you paddle around the north end of the island, head over to Hermitage Point, the large, low point of land directly ahead to the west, 0.5 mile distant. This point is covered with scattered trees and shrubs. You may see hikers or horseback riders on the trail that comes from Jackson Lake Lodge and Colter Bay and loops around this point. You can beach your boat anywhere along the shore if you want to explore the point for yourself, but if you head south you will soon come around the point to some nice beaches where you can also take-out easily and explore. The beaches make for good rest stops and give you more great views of the Tetons across the lake. The large island west of the point is Elk Island.

This is your turnaround point, having paddled about half of the 6-mile route, but if you are up for more paddling, head north along the west shore of Hermitage Point as far as you have time and energy for. The return route to the boat ramp can be done by retracing your steps north around Donoho Point and back to the ramp, or if the lake is calm enough you can shorten the trip by going around the south end of Donoho and paddling directly southeast to Signal Mountain. Always use great care when crossing open water. Waves can become dangerous.

26 Signal Mountain to Elk Island

Character: This trip of moderate length takes you by Donoho Point, Hermitage Point, and counterclockwise around the largest island on Jackson Lake, Elk Island. The island and the inlets and bays on its north side are fun to explore.

See map on page 115

Total paddling distance: 12 miles.
Average paddling time: 5–7 hours.
Put-in and take-out: Signal Mountain boat launch.
Difficulty: Moderate.
Be aware of: Afternoon winds and accompanying waves.
Attractions: Open water, island hopping, views of the Teton Range, some hiking, bird watching, fishing.
Maps: USGS 7.5-minute Moran–WY, Jenny Lake–WY.
Use: Light to moderate.
Directions: The turnoff for the Signal Mountain boat launch is located along Teton Park Road on the southeast shore of Jackson Lake, 3 miles south of Jackson Lake Junction and approximately 9 miles north of the Jenny Lake area. After turning west off the main road, follow the signs through the lodge area and development down to the large parking area and boat launch.

Taking a break on Hermitage Point, with a view of the Tetons to the southwest.

The paddling: This trip covers much of the south end of Jackson Lake. It combines island hopping with open-water paddling. The crossings are easily managed in calm waters. Read the description for trip 25 for details about the paddle around Donoho Point and on to Hermitage Point. Get an early start so that afternoon wind will pose less of a problem for your return.

When departing from the boat launch, you can either go north around Donoho Point, as previously described, or save some time and effort by going around the south end and more directly to Hermitage Point. The 12-mile total paddling distance listed here is the shortest route.

The crossing to Hermitage Point is a little less than 0.75 mile, depending on where you land. Be cautious of the weather and wind buildup. This is a short crossing, but all open-water crossings can become dangerous when winds increase. Use good sense and do not take chances if the weather is deteriorating. This advice should be heeded throughout the day as you get farther from the mainland.

Once you reach Hermitage Point, head along the west shore and around the sandy point. You can begin the 0.75-mile crossing to Elk Island here. As you are crossing, you may notice campers on the island. There are two sites on the southeast shore, one of which is reserved for groups.

Elk Island has a shoreline of about 6 miles. If you paddle north, or counterclockwise, you pass by large open meadows leading to one of the island's campsites, and as you continue north you'll see Dollar Island. Pass to the left, between the two islands and paddle along the wooded inlets of the north shore. There are convenient landing points all along this north shore. Look for waterfowl and shore-birds, along with the deer, elk, and bear that sometimes inhabit this island.

Mule deer, the most common deer in the region, are recognized by their rather large, broad ears and black-tipped tail. If alarmed, it bounds away with high, springing leaps, often clearing 4 vertical feet with each bound. The males produce an annual set of large, branched antlers which, when dropped, are often found by hikers. Leave them where they fell since they become a good source of calcium for rodents. Look for small gnawing marks, evidence of this fact.

Elk are the most common ungulate, or hooved mammal, in the region, num-bering roughly 100,000. Herds in the Yellowstone-Teton area are the largest in North America and can be found at all elevations throughout the summer months. In the fall, when the rut begins, they gradually move to lower elevations where magnificently antlered bulls can be heard bugling as they assemble a harem for breeding. The clash of antlers between competing males is often heard at quiet times. With the coming of snow, the cows and calves gather in herds, some num-bering in the hundreds, while the males wander off in much smaller groups to spend the winter.

Each winter thousands of elk die of starvation, a natural phenomenon. They become an important food source for coyotes, wolves, scavenging birds, and bears coming out of hibernation. Those that make it through the lean times live to see the snows retreat up the mountainsides, to give birth to fawns, and to begin the annual life cycle once again.

The west and south shores of Elk Island are more exposed than the rest of the island and less convenient for landing. They can also be swept by waves coming from the west, especially during afternoon hours. Unless conditions are extremely calm, paddle this stretch of the shoreline without much lingering. Don't miss the excellent views of the Tetons, though.

When crossing back from Elk Island to Hermitage or Donoho Point or the boat launch, use care. Pay attention to changing weather and the buildup of waves.

A word to the wise: It is far better to go ashore and wait out inclement conditions than to take unnecessary chances.

27 Signal Mountain to Elk Island and Moran Bay

Character: This long day trip takes you all the way across the south end of Jackson Lake and back | See map on page 115 |
along parts of the south shore, offering spectacular views of the Teton Range, particularly Mount Moran.
Total paddling distance: 14–16 miles.
Average paddling time: 7–9 hours.
Put-in and take-out: Signal Mountain boat launch.
Difficulty: Difficult.

Be aware of: Afternoon winds and accompanying waves, storm buildup, motorboat wakes.

Attractions: Open-water paddling on Jackson Lake, islands to explore, views of the Teton Range, bird watching, fishing.

Maps: USGS 7.5-minute Moran–WY, Jenny Lake–WY, Mt. Moran–WY.

Use: Light to moderate.

Directions: The turnoff for the Signal Mountain boat launch is located along Teton Park Road on the southeast shore of Jackson Lake, 3 miles south of Jackson Lake Junction and approximately 9 miles north of the Jenny Lake area. After turning west off the main road, follow the signs through the lodge area and development down to the large parking area and boat launch.

The paddling: This long day trip is an extension of trips 25 and 26, going all the way across the southern end of Jackson Lake into Moran Bay. Be sure to read those two descriptions for additional details. This description picks up at the west side of Elk Island.

Since this can be a long paddle, with several open-water stretches, know the weather forecast before heading out. When you reach the west side of Elk Island, you have paddled about 4.5 miles if you have gone the most direct route possible, farther if you paddled the northern shorelines of Donoho Point and Elk Island. You've reached an important decision point. Assess how you and your companions are doing and take a look at the weather. If you have enough energy and the

Moran Bay, with Mount Moran and Moran Canyon to the southwest.

wind and water remain calm, you can make a crossing to Moran Bay, but note that you've paddled less than halfway to your ultimate destination, the boat launch. The route ahead of you includes several long open-water crossings. If fatigue or weather dictates, head home from here.

If all conditions are a go and you decide to continue, cross to the point of land directly to the west. The crossing is about 1.25 miles, so use great caution, watching for wave buildup and possible wakes from passing motorboats. Pleasure boaters on Jackson Lake are generally considerate, but it is wise to keep a sharp eye for motorboats, sailboats, and jet skis.

Head just around the south end of the point to a small beach and a series of small meadows. The view in all directions is breathtaking. Wildflowers are usually thick and the Teton Range is in its full splendor, with Mount Moran looming overhead.

The mosaic of wildflowers in Yellowstone and Grand Teton is often dense and diverse, covering entire hillsides. As with all plants, even slight differences in soil moisture will be reflected in the presence of very different species of flowering plants. In wet-meadows, for example, look for the shooting star, a member of the primrose family. It is easily identified by its cluster of purple and lavender petals bent backward, exposing the colorful stamens. It is said to give the impression of speeding toward earth.

If you are paddling early in the season, look for the beautiful dogtooth violet, or glacier lily, as it is often referred to. Blooming soon after winter snows retreat, it is somewhat similar to the shooting star with its backward petals, but it is a bright yellow. Its underground bulb is a favorite food of bears. Also blooming as soon as snows melt is the pasqueflower, a single purple bloom surrounding a bright yellow pollen center, sitting atop a silky-haired stalk. *Pasque* refers to Paschal, or Easter season, when this plant is commonly in bloom.

In drier mountain meadows, arrowleaf balsamroot can be seen in vast blankets stretching out over the hillside. Growing up to 2 feet in height, its sunflower-like flowers are 2 to 4 inches across. This is a favorite of grazing wildlife, and Native Americans used the shoots, roots, and seeds as food. Another common flower of the meadow is the lupine, a 2- to-5-foot-tall plant having purple pea-like flowers. Look, too, for Indian paintbrush, a burst of narrow petals colored in bright red, yellow, or orange. The petals look as if their tips have been dipped in paint, hence the name.

To plan your return and know what to expect, study your map. Depending on water conditions, you have several options for the return to Signal Mountain. You can return the way you came or you can head to the point of land 1 mile south across Moran Bay, immediately east of Bearpaw Bay, and paddle east along the entire 8.5 miles of shore to the boat launch. This is the safest option.

Shortcuts can be considered if the weather is calm. You can cross the mouth of Spalding Bay, about 3 miles down the shore from Moran Bay, but it is nearly 1.25

miles wide. Use extreme caution. Another shortcut is to cross north at Deadman's Point over to the South Bar of Elk Island. This crossing is about 1 mile; then you're back in familiar territory, heading to Donoho Point and the boat launch.

Whatever route you choose, remember that this is a big lake where storms can develop suddenly. Use your best judgment and do not take chances. Wait out rough conditions or storms.

28 Colter Bay and Half Moon Bay

Character: This is a very pleasant paddle through and around the inlets, channels, and islands just south of Colter Bay. The route travels through several narrow, almost intimate channels and inlets on the way to Half Moon Bay, and then along stretches of the open lake approaching Little Mackinaw Bay, before heading back in to Colter Bay and the boat launch.

See map on page 115

Total paddling distance: 6 miles.
Average paddling time: 2–4 hours.
Put-in and take-out: Colter Bay boat launch.
Difficulty: Easy to moderate.
Be aware of: Afternoon winds and accompanying waves.
Attractions: Interesting shoreline with many inlets, narrow bays, and islands to explore, bird watching, fishing.
Map: USGS 7.5-minute Colter Bay–WY.
Use: Moderate, sometimes heavy around marina.
Directions: The Colter Bay area is located just off Teton Park Road, 4.2 miles north of Jackson Lake Lodge and 9 miles from Moran Junction. Turn into Colter Bay Village, following the signs to the marina and boat launch.

The paddling: This is a wonderful paddle through the protected inlets, narrow bays, and around the islands south of Colter Bay. The waterscape is an intimate one in a glacially carved, miniature fjordlike setting.

Colter Bay is named for John Colter, believed to be the first white person to enter the Teton-Yellowstone region. He had been with the Lewis and Clark Expedition from 1803 until his discharge in the summer of 1806. In 1807 and 1808 he made a now famous trek through the region in search of Indian tribes interested in trading at Manuel Lisa's trading post to the northeast on the Bighorn River in Montana. The fur trapper, 35 years old at the time, made the 500-mile tour through the region, much of which was in mountainous terrain, during the winter. He is also considered to be the first white person to see the wonders of Yellowstone.

As you head south out of Colter Bay, you paddle through the narrow opening between the mainland and the long point of land coming off the point of land forming the west side of the bay. Jackson Lake spreads before you. You can explore the narrow bay off to the east or cross its mouth and continue paddling south out of Colter Bay. Continue following the east shoreline around the bend through the narrow channel into Outlaw Bay and south through the even narrower channel 0.5 mile ahead. This channel connects Outlaw and Half Moon bays when the lake level is high enough.

After paddling through the narrow channel, you can go east or west around the island ahead and then into Half Moon Bay. Head west around the large unnamed island that has been to your right, or west, as you have moved south. Keep to the shoreline as you move around the southern lobe of the island, going between it and Sheffield Island to the south, and as you head north there will be a deep inlet straight ahead. This is another fun place to explore.

Continue north to Little Mackinaw Bay. Around the point of land ahead, to the north, is the beginning of Colter Bay and the return to the boat launch.

29 **Signal Mountain to Colter Bay**

Character: This trip offers a lot of variety as you See map on page 123 paddle north from the boat launch at Signal Mountain, around Hermitage Point, and through the protected inlets and channels eventually leading into Colter Bay. All or part of this route can be paddled since it is either round-trip or cut in half by a shuttle.
Total paddling distance: Up to 12 miles.
Average paddling time: 4–6 hours.
Put-in and take-out: Signal Mountain boat launch.
Difficulty: Moderate.
Be aware of: Afternoon winds and accompanying waves.
Attractions: Inlets, bays, and islands; fishing, bird life.
Maps: USGS 7.5-minute Moran–WY, Jenny Lake–WY, Colter Bay–WY.
Use: Light to moderate.
Directions: The turnoff for the Signal Mountain boat launch is located along Teton Park Road on the southeast shore of Jackson Lake, 3 miles south of Jackson Lake Junction and approximately 9 miles north of the Jenny Lake area. After turning west off the main road, follow the signs through the lodge area and development down to the large parking area and boat launch.

The paddling: The entire round trip is 12 miles. Options include paddling the route in reverse on the return or making arrangements for a shuttle pickup at Colter Bay, cutting the trip in half. Views of the Teton Range are spectacular throughout and the wildflowers are equally magnificent.

Launch at Signal Mountain boat launch and head west around the south end of both Donoho Point and Hermitage Point, then north to Colter Bay. Read the descriptions for trips 25 and 28 for paddling details out of Signal Mountain and in Colter Bay, the midway destination. Heading north along the west shore of Hermitage Point, you come to a small bay, less than 0.5 mile across, with a little peninsula poking out to the northwest at its north side. This bay is more than half the paddling distance to Colter Bay. Keep a keen eye for eagles and ospreys.

Jackson Lake

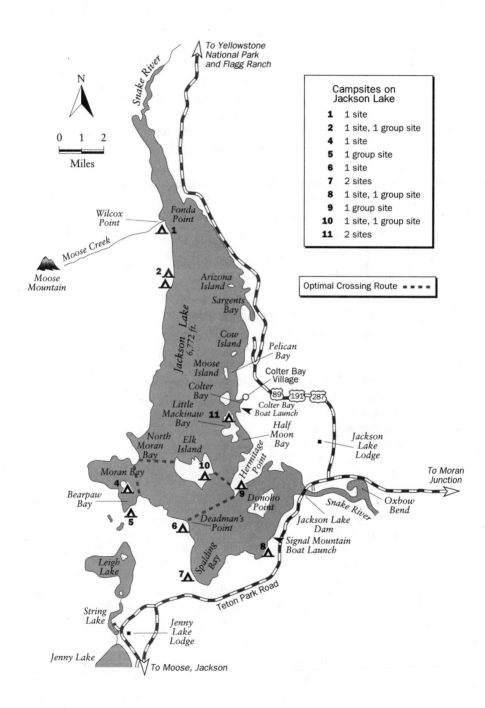

To Yellowstone
National Park
and Flagg Ranch

Snake River

N

0   1   2

Miles

Wilcox
Point

Fonda
Point

△ 1

Moose Creek

Moose
Mountain

△ 2

Arizona
Island

Sargents
Bay

Jackson Lake 6,772 ft.

Cow
Island

Pelican
Bay

Moose
Island

Colter Bay
Village

Colter
Bay

89 191 287

Little
Mackinaw
Bay

△ 11

Colter Bay
Boat Launch

Half
Moon
Bay

Jackson
Lake
Lodge

North
Moran
Bay

Elk
Island

△ 10

Hermitage Point

Moran Bay

△ 4

△ 9

Donoho
Point

To Moran
Junction

Bearpaw
Bay

△ 5

△ 6

*Deadman's
Point*

Snake River

Oxbow
Bend

Jackson Lake
Dam

Spalding Bay

△ 8

Signal Mountain
Boat Launch

Leigh
Lake

△ 7

String
Lake

Teton Park Road

Jenny
Lake
Lodge

Jenny Lake

To Moose, Jackson

**Campsites on
Jackson Lake**

1	1 site
2	1 site, 1 group site
4	1 site
5	1 group site
6	1 site
7	2 sites
8	1 site, 1 group site
9	1 group site
10	1 site, 1 group site
11	2 sites

Optimal Crossing Route ▪ ▪ ▪ ▪

The remainder of the route goes through the small inlets and channels of Half Moon and Colter bays and is very different from any other paddling in the area. Trip 28 gives you a good idea of what to expect with the route in this calmer, protected area but describes it from the opposite direction. You stand a chance of seeing moose, deer, and elk, as well as various water birds.

Once you paddle around the little peninsula mentioned above, you enter Half Moon Bay. Stick to the east shore, or paddle out to the west of the island at the north side of the bay. Either way will take you to the very narrow channel farther north. Passing through this and another channel 0.5 mile north brings you into Colter Bay. The boat launch is at the end of the bay to the east. If you have a shuttle arranged, you end the trip at this point. Otherwise, head back south the way you came. Trip 28 describes the route.

For greater variety, when you exit Colter Bay, continue paddling across the inlet to the south, then head west around the large island into Little Mackinaw Bay. Be prepared to be exposed to large waves; use extreme caution.

If conditions are unstable, stick to the shoreline, following it south into Half Moon Bay and around Hermitage Point and retracing your route to the boat launch at Signal Mountain.

30 Colter Bay to Sargents Bay

Character: This trip takes you north along the open east shore of Jackson Lake, with some exploring into larger inlets.

See map on page 123

Total paddling distance: 11 miles.
Average paddling time: 4–6 hours.
Put-in and take-out: Colter Bay boat launch.
Difficulty: Moderate.
Be aware of: Afternoon winds and accompanying waves.
Attractions: A taste of big lake paddling, while staying close to shore, bird watching, fishing.
Map: USGS 7.5-minute Colter Bay–WY.
Use: Moderate.
Directions: The Colter Bay area is located just off Teton Park Road, 4.2 miles north of Jackson Lake Lodge and 9 miles from Moran Junction. Turn into Colter Bay Village, following the signs to the marina and boat launch.

The paddling: This is a good trip for those seeking more of a big lake, open-water paddle, traveling as far north as desired before returning to Colter Bay. Unlike the more protected route of trip 25, this one follows the open shoreline of Jackson Lake, with exposure to winds and waves that can build up across the open stretches to the west. Use caution and stay near shore.

After paddling through the relatively protected Colter Bay, continue around the large lobe of land to your right, and head north into Jackson Lake, sticking to the shoreline as much as necessary as you head north. You pass by the large Colter Bay campground on the slope to the east. In about 2 miles you come into Pelican Bay, with Moose Island to the west. After passing through the bay, the shoreline heads in to the east. Leek's Marina is just to the north and Cow Island is to the west. At Leek's Marina you are about 1.5 miles from the mouth of Sargents Bay, which cuts back to the southeast a half mile. If the water has been rough, the bay will be a welcome haven.

Sargents Bay is the somewhat arbitrary midway destination of this trip; a longer or shorter paddle is at your discretion.

SNAKE RIVER

Originating in the mountains near the southern end of Yellowstone Park, the Snake River, with all its meanders and side channels, provides varied and essential habitat for a diversity of plant, bird, and mammal life. Cottonwood trees, willow, and aspen trees line the bank. Ospreys, eagles, pelicans, and waterfowl can be viewed throughout the two segments of the river described here and it is not unusual for paddlers to also see moose, beavers, otters, and muskrats. Trout abound.

The Snake River can be quite powerful, cold, and swift along certain stretches and at any time of the year, especially during the spring snow melt. Inexperienced paddlers should not attempt this river, except perhaps in the slower moving current of the Oxbow Bend area just downstream from the Jackson Lake Dam. Always read the current river conditions posted at launch site bulletin boards, or contact a ranger station for specifics.

This guide describes two segments of the river: the section north of Jackson Lake and south of Flagg Ranch, and the section below the Jackson Lake Dam to Pacific Creek.

Remember that arranging your own shuttle between put-ins and take-outs is necessary.

31 Flagg Ranch to Lizard Creek Campground

Character: This intermediate paddle floats the often complicated braided channel of the Snake River for 6 miles before entering the north end of Jackson Lake and following the lakeshore to Lizard Creek.

See map on page 127

Total paddling distance: 10 miles.
Average paddling time: 4–5 hours.
Put-in: Flagg Ranch boat landing.
Take-out: Lizard Creek Campground.
Difficulty: Moderate/intermediate to difficult/advanced.
Be aware of: Sometimes confusing to find the route; rock, boulder field, and gravel bar obstacles, river debris; strong river currents.
Attractions: Quick, often exciting current, many islands, lake paddle, views of the Teton Range.

The Flagg Ranch boat launch on the Snake River.

Maps: USGS 7.5-minute Flagg Ranch–WY, Colter Bay–WY.
Use: Moderate to heavy.
Directions: The Flagg Ranch boat landing, or launch, is located 2.4 miles south of the South Entrance of Yellowstone Park, south of the Flagg Ranch Village resort, at the highway bridge. This is on the John D. Rockefeller Jr. Memorial Parkway, about 5 miles north of the Teton National Park border, or 21 miles north of the Colter Bay area.

The paddling: This day trip includes a 6-mile float on a remote stretch of the Snake River and a 4-mile paddle along the northeast shore of Jackson Lake to the take-out at Lizard Creek Campground. The float down the Snake River, paralleling the John D. Rockefeller Jr. Memorial Parkway, can be exciting as you negotiate the best route through the often confusing braided channel. There are several islands and many gravel bars, boulder fields, snags, and piles of river debris to contend with, making this stretch of the river manageable for paddlers of at least intermediate skill level. Be sure to carefully read the current river conditions, which are posted on a bulletin board at the Flagg Ranch boat landing. Consult the route map in this book and at the launch, so you can best anticipate what to expect.

John D. Rockefeller Jr. had a long, very productive history in the Teton area. After a 1926 tour of the region, he began to purchase lands in Jackson Hole, the broad, flat valley lying east of the Teton Range. Eventually buying more than 35,000 acres in the valley and north to Yellowstone Park, he was able to give these to the United States government in 1949 after years of political maneuvering. In 1972, the John D. Rockefeller Jr. Memorial Parkway was established to

Snake River,
Flagg Ranch to Lizard Creek Campground

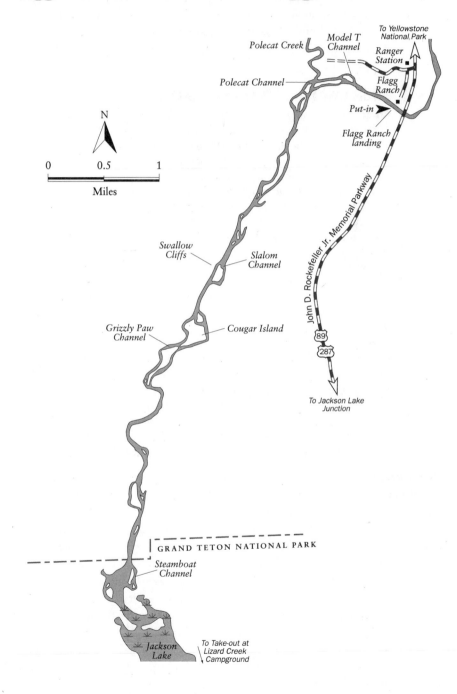

N

0   0.5   1

Miles

Polecat Creek

Model T Channel

To Yellowstone National Park

Ranger Station

Flagg Ranch

Polecat Channel

Put-in

Flagg Ranch landing

Swallow Cliffs

Slalom Channel

John D. Rockefeller Jr. Memorial Parkway

Grizzly Paw Channel

Cougar Island

89

287

To Jackson Lake Junction

GRAND TETON NATIONAL PARK

Steamboat Channel

Jackson Lake

To Take-out at Lizard Creek Campground

127

commemorate his significant contributions to the cause of conservation.

When you enter the upper north end of Jackson Lake, expect to find varied depths and boggy conditions at times as the river channel enters its deltalike setting. Follow the east shoreline 4 miles to Lizard Creek Campground. Remember that prevailing winds from the southwest can often result in large waves on the lake, especially along the shoreline at this end.

32 Jackson Lake Dam to Pacific Creek

Character: This is a calm trip through the Oxbow
Bend area, which is famous for its views of the Teton

See map on page 129

Range. Varied birdlife, including eagles, ospreys, pelicans, and
waterfowl, can be expected along the route, in addition to signs of
beaver and the occasional otter.

Total paddling distance: 5 miles.

Average paddling time: 2–4 hours.

Put-in: Jackson Lake Dam.

Take-out: Pacific Creek Landing.

Difficulty: Easy to moderate/intermediate.

Be aware of: A few river obstacles, no shore access at eagle nesting
areas, swifter current at Pacific Creek take-out.

Attractions: Oxbow Bend scenic area; ospreys, pelicans, moose,
otter, beavers, fishing.

Map: USGS 7.5-minute Moran–WY.

Use: Light to moderate.

Directions: The put-in at Jackson Lake Dam is located by turning
south on the short road just north of the dam. From the east it is 1
mile west of Jackson Lake Junction on Teton Park Road. Park toward
the east end of the parking area near the bulletin board. The take-out
at the Pacific Creek launch parking lot is 4.6 miles from the put-in
road, east down Teton Park Road toward Moran Junction, which is
another 0.25 mile farther down the road from the lot.

The paddling: This stretch of the Snake River, due to its calmer current and minimal obstacles, is ideal for beginning and intermediate paddlers. Portions of the river are almost lakelike, while other short stretches have a quicker, more powerful current but are still easy to negotiate. A side trip through the famous Oxbow Bend area allows you to experience this "calendar quality" scene in the intimate manner available only to paddlers.

The water throughout is exceedingly clear, and views of fish are always possible as you paddle along. Water birds are common, as are eagles, ospreys, and pelicans. Eagles nest along the river, and portions of the riverbank are closed to access to protect nesting sites. Watch for posted signs.

After putting in just below the Jackson Lake Dam, you move quickly downstream in a deep, strong current. Anglers are common along this stretch as they try their skill on the native Snake River cutthroat trout. Do your best to stay out of

Snake River,
Jackson Lake Dam to Pacific Creek

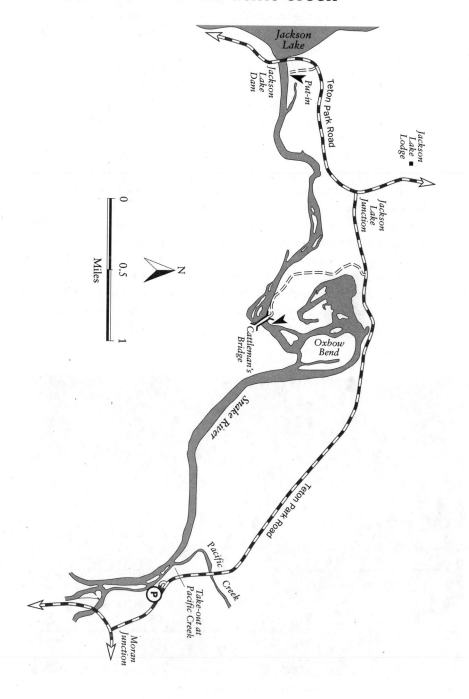

their way by moving to the other side of the river. Pelicans can often be seen "fishing" in this area, too. Give them the space they need to feed undisturbed.

Within about 20 to 30 minutes, or 2 miles, you come to an old bridge, Cattleman's Bridge, crossing the Snake. This bridge may be removed in the near future, but in the meantime the bridge pilings and the bridge's relatively low span can be obstacles to avoid in higher water; a portage around this bridge allows you to avoid these potential hazards. There is a launch on the left bank, immediately upstream of this bridge, accessible from Teton Park Road via a 1-mile dirt road.

After passing Cattleman's Bridge, keep left of the island just ahead in order to reach Oxbow Bend. If you float to the right you will pass through smaller, shallower channels.

Rivers are dynamic, changing, and evolving through time. Young rivers flow fast and relatively straight as they cut downward through steep terrain from their origins. As they age, rivers gradually change the valley through which they flow. Eroded sediment is carried downstream and deposited, gradually leveling the valley floor. As the river slows, it also begins to meander a bit. The water moves more quickly on the outside bends of the river and more slowly on the inside curves. This results in a carving away of the outside riverbank. Inversely, the slower current on the inside curves deposits more sediment from upstream, thereby building up that portion of the stream channel. What once was a straight flowing river takes on exaggerated bends. Eventually the river, seeking the most direct route to lower elevations, breaks a shortcut through the land instead of following the

The scenic Oxbow Bend makes a side trip through here a wise option.

meandering curve. What previously was the bed of the river becomes an oxbow of quiet water, detached from the main current.

These areas of slow water attract different plants and animals. Rooted aquatic plants take hold here, and the slower water encourages algae growth. Animal life becomes more diverse, too, as one-celled plankton find it easier to survive in the calmer water, and beaver, otter, muskrat, and a variety of waterfowl find a preferred habitat here.

After floating out of Oxbow Bend, you pass through more calm waters. Look for beaver lodges and any residents that may be at work. About 3 miles from Cattleman's Bridge, Pacific Creek enters from the left.

Pacific Creek flows out of the Teton Wilderness, northeast of Teton Park and south of Yellowstone Park. Two Ocean Divide, to the north, is part of the Continental Divide, the great north-south range of mountains that divides water flow into the Pacific or Atlantic oceans. The water flowing in Pacific Creek soon mingles with the waters of the Snake River, whose waters eventually flow into the Pacific Ocean.

The current picks up considerably where Pacific Creek joins the Snake River. The take-out is just a short way downstream from here. At high water, paddling into the take-out may be tricky. Look for quiet waters upstream of the take-out in which to beach your boat.

The take-out area is actually about 100 yards upstream of the parking lot, which can't be seen from the river.

Multi-day trips

33 String Lake to Leigh Lake

See map on page 104

Character: This trip gives you a taste of the Teton backcountry on a lake very manageable for even the novice paddler. The views of the Teton Range, in particular Mount Moran, are truly spectacular.

Total paddling distance: 7 miles.

Suggested time: 2 days.

Put-in and take-out: String Lake boat launch.

Difficulty: Easy.

Campsites: No. 16 or no. 14

Be aware of: Afternoon wind and accompanying waves, precautions for food storage in bear country.

Attractions: Easy paddling on an easily accessible lake, spectacular views of the Teton Range, fishing.

Map: USGS 7.5-minute Jenny Lake–WY.

Use: Moderate.

Directions: The parking lot of the String Lake Trailhead is located by turning west off Teton Park Road at North Jenny Lake Junction. Follow the signs to Jenny Lake Lodge and String Lake, about 3 miles down the road. Just before the lodge, the road to the boat launch bears right, dead-ending at String Lake.

The boat launch at String Lake.

The paddling: Paddling the 2 miles across Leigh Lake, with its views of the Teton Range to the west, is a wonderful way to get into the backcountry with minimal effort. The moderate size of Leigh Lake makes it appealing to those with limited time or to novice paddlers fearful of committing to a more arduous overnight experience. Read descriptions for trips 21 and 23 for greater detail about what to expect in the way of paddling along String Lake, the short portage to Leigh Lake, and what Leigh Lake itself has to offer.

From the end of the portage, paddle past Boulder Island, following the west shore of the lake around to one of the two campsites (number 14 or number 16) at the far west end of the lake. Both of these sites, one situated at the base of Paintbrush Canyon and the other at the base of Leigh Canyon, are in heavy trees with great views of the lake. Site number 14 is just above lake level, while number 16 is up on the bank in the trees.

If you get an early start, there is ample time to explore the entire shoreline of Leigh Lake, to go fishing, or to hike into the canyons.

The trails in this area pass through dense spruce-fir forests. Look for the female cone of the Douglas-fir, identified by the featherlike bracts growing between the cone scales. The bracts look very much like the tail and legs of a miniature mouse hiding in the scales. This fir is not a true fir. True firs, like the subalpine fir, also growing nearby, have purplish cones that grow upright from the higher branches much like candles.

In and around the rushing waters, look for the American dipper, or water ouzel, a nondescript gray bird, smaller than a robin, that bobs constantly and can be seen walking into the swiftest of currents in search of water insects and their larvae.

34 **Signal Mountain to Elk Island**

Character: This overnight trip is a big lake experience spent exploring part of the south end of Jackson Lake, with a night spent on Elk Island. The views of the Tetons are impressive throughout the trip.

See map on page 115

Total paddling distance: 6 miles.

Suggested time: 2 days.

Put-in and take-out: Signal Mountain boat launch.

Difficulty: Moderate.

Campsite: No. 10.

Be aware of: Afternoon winds and accompanying waves; precautions for food storage in bear country.

Attractions: Island camping and exploring, fishing.

Map: USGS 7.5-minute Jenny Lake–WY.

Use: Light to moderate.

Directions: The turnoff for the Signal Mountain boat launch is located along Teton Park Road on the southeast shore of Jackson Lake, 3 miles south of Jackson Lake Junction and approximately 9 miles north of the Jenny Lake area. After turning west off the main

Along the way to Elk Island, a stop at Donoho Point provides a stunning view.

road, follow the signs through the lodge area and development down to the large parking area and boat launch.

The paddling: This short trip features open-water crossings up to 0.75 mile and island camping. The views, as everywhere on this lake, are beautiful panoramic vistas of one of the great mountain backdrops in the world. Refer to the descriptions for trips 25 and 26 for greater details about what to expect on Jackson Lake.

Your destination is Elk Island in the middle of the south end of Jackson Lake. There are two campsites on the island, both located on the southeast side directly west of Hermitage Point. One of the sites is reserved for parties of 7 to 12 people. The site for individual parties, number 10, is located on a sunny, grassy slope in the midst of scattered trees. The views from this camp are to the east, and the morning sun strikes this camp early.

While there are no designated trails on the island, some good day hikes are possible. The high point of the island is 6,918 feet, about 150 feet above the water surface, and provides nice views of the lake. A circumnavigation of the island can be fun, too. The north shore of the island has protected inlets with easy access to land. The west and south shores, however, can be swept with large waves. Be careful.

35 String Lake to Leigh Lake

Character: This lake is large enough to provide 3-day experiences, especially for those wanting a relaxed backcountry stay with plenty of time to explore the shore, to hike, or to fish.

See map on page 104

Total paddling distance: Approximately 7 miles.
Suggested time: 3 days.
Put-in and take-out: String Lake boat launch.
Difficulty: Easy.
Campsites: No. 12, no. 13, or no. 15.
Be aware of: Afternoon wind and accompanying waves, precautions for food storage in bear country.
Attractions: Easy paddling on an easily accessible lake, spectacular views of the Teton Range, fishing.
Map: USGS 7.5-minute Jenny Lake–WY.
Use: Moderate.
Directions: The parking lot of the String Lake Trailhead is located by turning west off Teton Park Road at North Jenny Lake Junction. Follow the signs to Jenny Lake Lodge and String Lake, about 3 miles down the road. Just before the lodge, the road to the boat launch bears right, dead-ending at String Lake.

The paddling: This 3-day trip into Leigh Lake is a straightforward paddle similar to the ones in trips 23 and 33. Since Leigh Lake is relatively small, about 2 miles long, and has a limited number of campsites, the options for a multi-day trip are fairly evident. Since backcountry campers are permitted to stay at a site for two

Exploring the west end of Leigh Lake.

consecutive nights, you can always use this option in designing a 3-day trip. The layover day can be used to explore the shoreline and surrounding land.

On the other hand, you can break camp and move to a new site for the second night. This gives you the opportunity to experience the lake and the surrounding mountains from a different perspective. For example, staying in a site at the west end of the lake allows you to get the morning sun often before other sites, but the mountain views to the west can be limited. On the other hand, choosing site number 12 on the east shore or site number 15 on the southwest shore provides a much better vantage point from which to view the mountains. Site number 13, also on the southwest shore, has a nice beach. The choice is yours!

36 Signal Mountain to south end of Jackson Lake

Character: The south end of Jackson Lake is a good destination for those with limited time who want to see a varied waterscape and landscape. The lake's waters can stay relatively calm due to the westerly direction of prevailing winds.

See map on page 123

Total paddling distance: 11 miles.
Suggested time: 3 days.
Put-in and take-out: Signal Mountain boat launch.
Difficulty: Moderate to difficult.
Campsites: No. 6 and no. 10.
Be aware of: Afternoon winds and accompanying waves; precautions for food storage in bear country.
Attractions: Big lake paddling with islands and points of land to provide safety, island camping and exploring, fishing.
Maps: USGS 7.5-minute Jenny Lake–WY.
Use: Light to moderate.
Directions: The turnoff for the Signal Mountain boat launch is located along Teton Park Road on the southeast shore of Jackson Lake, 3 miles south of Jackson Lake Junction and approximately 9 miles north of the Jenny Lake area. After turning west off the main road, follow the signs through the lodge area and development down to the large parking area and boat launch.

The paddling: This 3-day trip travels into the extreme south end of Jackson Lake, moving clockwise, paddling out to Elk Island, and returning to the Signal Mountain boat launch.

The first day is a simple, 8-mile trip from the boat launch at Signal Mountain south along the shore into Spalding Bay and around to camp number 6, Deadman's Point. Views of the mountains are somewhat hidden at this site, but lake views to the north are unobstructed.

Day two can involve a leisurely trip to Elk Island with plenty of time to explore or a longer paddle into Moran Bay to the northwest before heading to Elk Island

and then back to your camp at Deadman's.

A word to the wise: The crossing to Elk Island is one mile from Deadman's Point and 1.5 miles from Moran Bay. Making these crossings earlier in the day usually ensures calmer conditions.

If crossing from Deadman's Point to Elk Island, you come to South Bar, Elk Island's point of land extending to the south. Use great care in all lake crossings, watching wind, waves, and the weather carefully. Once you reach the point, paddle less than 0.5 mile to the north side of the small bay to the west until you see the number 10 site marker in the meadow above the lake. Read the description for trips 26 and 34 for greater detail about Elk Island.

You should have ample time to explore the island by water or land. If you plan to explore the shore, remember that afternoon waves can be high along the south shore of the island. Travel with great care, staying close to shore, or waiting out rough or stormy conditions.

Day three is an eastward trip, 0.75 mile across to Hermitage Point, where you can head south around Donoho Point to the southeast and on to the boat launch. Alternately, after reaching Hermitage Point, you can paddle north along the east shore of Hermitage Point, cross to Donoho Point at its north end, and come around the east shore of the island, before crossing to the boat launch. This route is a little more protected in rough weather.

37 Signal Mountain to south end of Jackson Lake

See map on page 123

Character: This trip covers most of the south end of the lake, taking you through open water, protected inlets and bays, and around several islands, camping on three of them. A 5-day variation is included at the end of the description.

Total paddling distance: 20 miles.

Suggested time: 4–5 days.

Put-in and take-out: Signal Mountain boat launch.

Difficulty: Moderate to difficult.

Suggested campsites: No. 11, no. 4, and no. 6.

Be aware of: Afternoon winds and accompanying waves; precautions for food storage in bear country.

Attractions: Big lake paddling with islands and points of land to provide safety, island camping and exploring, fishing.

Map: USGS 7.5-minute Jenny Lake–WY.

Use: Light to moderate.

Directions: The turnoff for the Signal Mountain boat launch is located along Teton Park Road on the southeast shore of Jackson Lake, 3 miles south of Jackson Lake Junction and approximately 9 miles north of the Jenny Lake area. After turning west off the main road, follow the signs through the lodge area and development down to the large parking area and boat launch.

The paddling: The first day of paddling takes you from Signal Mountain boat launch 5 miles north to Little Mackinaw Bay on the north lobe of a large island just south of Colter Bay. Read trips 28 and 29 for details about this route through the many bays, inlets, and channels in the island group. The most direct route to Little Mackinaw Bay is along the west side of the island. If water conditions in this area are rough, take the more protected route through the channels on the east side of the island, and come around to the bay from the north side. The camp, number 11, on the north side of Little Mackinaw Bay, gives you a wonderful view of the Teton Range to the south and west.

Day two is a 7-mile journey, retracing some of the previous day's route, and includes two open-water crossings. After breaking camp, head south along the west side of the island, around the south end, crossing Half Moon Bay toward the north end of Hermitage Point. Along this point you must choose the best place to cross west to Elk Island. The narrowest crossing is 0.75 mile at the south end of the point. Crossing more to the north can be at least a mile. Use great care in making your choice of crossing, consulting your map for specifics and watching the weather and water conditions carefully.

Once you get to Elk Island, travel counterclockwise to the north shore. Trip 26 will give you additional details about Elk Island, and trip 27 explains the next crossing you have to make. As you paddle around Elk Island, pause on the west side to prepare for the 1.5-mile crossing west to the point at Moran Bay. This is a long and potentially dangerous crossing. As with all lake crossings, assess carefully what you are about to undertake.

At this point, the second night's camp (number 4) is about 0.75 mile away, on Little Grassy Island to the south. If time permits, and you have the energy, an exploration of the north shoreline of the bay is recommended. The views of the mountains and canyons from this perspective are spectacular. The camp on Little Grassy Island is wonderful, sitting below the massive mountains standing just to the west.

The third day of this trip is the short 3-mile shoreline paddle east to camp number 6 at Deadman's Point. You have plenty of time to get a leisurely start and explore more of the shore to the west before heading east to camp. When you depart Little Grassy Island, head south along the scattered islands and either into Bearpaw Bay or across its mouth. Continue east along the open and burned slopes to the south, looking for the site marker of camp number 6. This is your last evening on Jackson Lake.

Your final day requires a 4-mile paddle back to the boat launch. You may want to review trip 27 for more specifics. The route is straightforward, weather permitting, and includes three open-water crossings, one of which is a mile in

Kayaks pulled up on the shore of Moran Bay with Little Grassy Island in the distance.

length. If conditions cause you concern (perhaps you woke to inclement weather and high winds), review trip 27 for the various alternatives to an open-water crossing. Use your best judgment and do not take chances. It is far better to paddle the longer shoreline route than to risk even the shortest open-water crossing in rough water.

Reserving two nights at a particular site gives you a 5-day variation of this trip. To do so at Little Grassy Island, for instance, gives you a layover day to explore the Moran Bay area.

38 Colter Bay to west side of Jackson Lake

Character: This multi-day trip, the length of which is up to you, takes you along the less traveled west shore of Jackson Lake. Depending on your choice of several possible put-ins, this trip can also involve a float on the Snake River. A shuttle will be required in some cases if you don't want to retrace your steps to the put-in. A loop trip is described here.

See map on page 123

Total paddling distance: Approximately 30–40 miles, depending on the route selected.

Suggested time: 4 days or more.

Put-in and take-out: Colter Bay boat launch, or other described options.

Difficulty: Difficult.

Campsites: Nos. 1, 2, 4, 6, 7, 8, 10, and 11.

Be aware of: Afternoon winds and accompanying waves; precautions for food storage in bear country.

Attractions: An exploration of the relatively wild west shore, possible Snake River float, fishing.

Maps: USGS 7.5-minute Jenny Lake–WY, Colter Bay–WY, Flagg Ranch–WY.

Use: Light to moderate.

Directions: The Colter Bay area is located just off Teton Park Road, 4.2 miles north of Jackson Lake Lodge, and 9 miles from Moran Junction. Turn into Colter Bay Village, following the signs to the marina and boat ramp.

The paddling: This exploration of the northern half of the lake includes most of the west shore and takes you into less visited areas. It involves some long days of paddling, but you'll have experienced a great deal of this magnificent lake when you are done.

The put-in for this trip is the Colter Bay boat launch. The first day is a long one, 12 miles, and an early start is important so you arrive at camp before gusty winds create large waves, a common afternoon occurrence. Review trip 30 for details of the route from Colter Bay north to Sargents Bay. Stay close to shore to avoid open-water wind and wave problems. You pass to the east of Moose and Cow islands on your way to the mouth of Sargents Bay, 5 miles from Colter Bay.

Continuing north past the mouth of this bay, you paddle past several more bays and to the east of Arizona Island. Within about 2 miles, Teton Park Road begins to run parallel to the lakeshore for more than 2 miles. At Fonda Point, just ahead, the lake narrows to about 0.5 mile, and you see Lizard Creek Campground on the east shore.

This is where you make the crossing to the west shore. Prevailing winds from the southwest often result in a buildup of large waves in this area. If water conditions are safe for crossing, do so along this stretch. Otherwise continue north until you reach a narrower and safer crossing.

Once you cross to the west shore, paddle south about 0.5 mile, depending on where you crossed, to Wilcox Point and camp number 1. This, your first night's camp, is a beautiful, remote one. It is at the base of the mountains, with views to the north and east. The small bay next to camp is at the mouth of Webb Canyon, cut by Moose Creek coming off Moose Mountain, which towers almost 3,500 feet above the lake. The nearness of the mountains limits west shore campsites to just two: number 1 at Wilcox Point and number 2 at Warm Springs, 2.75 miles south, another great site with meadows of wildflowers and good views in almost all directions.

On day two you continue paddling south 10 miles to your second night's camp on Little Grassy Island. A sense of great wildness pervades the route. Colter and Waterfall canyons drop out of the steep slopes, draining unseen snow fields. A review of trip 37 will give you an idea of what to expect from Little Grassy Island and the southern end of the lake.

From the island, you are approximately 9 miles from Colter Bay by the most direct route of Deadman's Point to Hermitage Point and on north to Half Moon and Colter bays. This is a reasonable day-paddle, considering what distance you've covered so far, but you may want to lengthen the trip by staying another night or two on the lake. A layover on Little Grassy Island would allow a good visit into the southwest end of the lake and an exploration of the steep canyons draining into Moran Bay. If time permits, longer shoreline exploration would certainly provide a more in-depth backcountry experience.

A complete shoreline circumnavigation of the lake is a manageable goal. From Little Grassy Island, you can continue along the south end of the lake, around to the Signal Mountain area, and back north to Colter Bay, a total of 17 to 18 miles of paddling. There are camps scattered along the entire route. Campsite number 6, at Deadman's Point, is 3 miles from Little Grassy Island. Spalding Bay, number 7, is another 2 miles down the shore, with number 8, South Landing, on the southeast shore 6 miles farther along.

From here campsites become more sparse. Elk Island's number 10 is 4 miles from number 7, with several lake crossings. This is the more direct route, paddling south of Donoho Point and out to Hermitage Point, before crossing to Elk Island. Between Elk Island and Colter Bay there is one more site, number 11 at Little

The north end of Jackson Lake near the mouth of the Snake River.

Mackinaw Bay, about 4 miles away.

If a shuttle arrangement can be made, this trip could start with a 4-mile float down the Snake River beginning at the Flagg Ranch boat landing before paddling along the west shore to camp number 1 or number 2. Starting a trip there requires a shuttle pickup at either Signal Mountain or Colter Bay.

Appendix

BOAT PERMITS AND WATERCRAFT USE

For questions regarding watercraft use in Yellowstone National Park, contact the Visitor Services Office (VSO) at 307-344-2107. For Grand Teton National Park, call 307-739-3399, or for a recording to receive a general information packet, call 307-739-3600.

BACKCOUNTRY CAMPING

In Yellowstone National Park. For a complete and detailed description of backcountry use of the Yellowstone Lake area, including all policies, procedures, and campsite locations, consult the "Backcountry Trip Planner," available by calling 307-344-2160 or by writing Yellowstone National Park, Central Backcountry Office, P.O. Box 168, Yellowstone Park, WY 82190.

In Grand Teton National Park. To receive the "Backcountry Camping" brochure, which explains all policies and procedures and shows campsite locations on maps, write to Grand Teton National Park, Permits Office, P.O. Drawer 170, Moose, WY 83012 or call 307-739-3309 or 307-739-3397.

For reservations write to the permits office or fax them at 307-739-3438. If you choose to make a reservation in person, make it between 8 A.M. and 5 P.M. at the Moose Visitor Center, just west of Moose Junction, the intersection of Teton Park Road and U.S. Highway 89/26/191 (the John D. Rockefeller Jr. Parkway). After May 15, you have no choice; reservations must be made in person at the Moose Visitor Center within 24 hours of your departure. Backcountry Use Permits may be picked up at both the Moose and Colter Bay visitor centers, or at the Jenny Lake Ranger Station.

TAKING THE SHUTTLE

For information and schedules, call 307-344-7311 year-round, or during the summer months, call the Bridge Bay Marina at 307-242-3880.

MAP PUBLISHERS

USGS maps are available from many outdoor equipment stores and map specialty stores in your area. Look in the Yellow Pages under *maps, commercial dealers.* They can also be ordered directly from the United States Geological Survey (USGS) Map Distribution Center, Box 25046 Denver Fed Ctr, Denver CO 80225. Computer access is through the web at www.usgs.gov/major_sites.html.

Trails Illustrated maps are available by mail from P.O. Box 4357, Evergreen, CO 80437-4357, or by phone at 800-962-1643. Computer access is by e-mail at topomaps@aol.com, or via the web at www.colorado.com/trails.

Index

Page numbers in *italics* refer to photo captions.

About the Author

The author at Lake Butte Overlook, above Yellowstone Lake. PHOTO BY SHEILA KOERNER

For more than 35 years, **Don Nelson** has been fortunate to spend much of his life in the outdoors.

Canoeing and backpacking in Ohio, Pennsylvania, and Canada in the 1960s became the foundation for a diverse career in the outdoors. In the early 1970s he organized and led backpack trips for Newman Outfitters in Cleveland, Ohio.

After moving to Colorado to lead backpack and horse trips, Don worked for Holubar Mountaineering in Boulder. He then spent nine years in Boulder with The National Audubon Society in several capacities, including Rocky Mountain Regional Representative, and director of Audubon Camp in the West.

In the late 1980s, he became a teacher and started a public alternative middle school program in Boulder, Colorado before moving to Yellowstone National Park, where he directed the nonprofit Yellowstone Institute for six years.

In addition to his paddling interests, Don is an avid hiker, cross-country skier, and woodworker, having built furniture and cedar strip canoes.

FALCONGUIDES ® Leading the Way™

FALCONGUIDES ® are available for where-to-go hiking, mountain biking, rock climbing, walking, scenic driving, fishing, rockhounding, paddling, birding, wildlife viewing, and camping. We also have FalconGuides on essential outdoor skills and subjects and field identification. The following titles are currently available, but this list grows every year. For a free catalog with a complete list of titles, call FALCON toll-free at 1-800-582-2665.

HIKING GUIDES

Hiking Alaska
Hiking Arizona
Hiking Arizona's Cactus Country
Hiking the Beartooths
Hiking Big Bend National Park
Hiking the Bob Marshall Country
Hiking California
Hiking California's Desert Parks
Hiking Carlsbad Caverns
   and Guadalupe Mtns. National Parks
Hiking Colorado
Hiking Colorado, Vol.II
Hiking Colorado's Summits
Hiking Colorado's Weminuche Wilderness
Hiking the Columbia River Gorge
Hiking Florida
Hiking Georgia
Hiking Glacier & Waterton Lakes National Parks
Hiking Grand Canyon National Park
Hiking Grand Staircase-Escalante/Glen Canyon
Hiking Grand Teton National Park
Hiking Great Basin National Park
Hiking Hot Springs in the Pacific Northwest
Hiking Idaho
Hiking Maine
Hiking Michigan
Hiking Minnesota
Hiking Montana
Hiking Mount Rainier National Park
Hiking Mount St. Helens
Hiking Nevada
Hiking New Hampshire

Hiking New Mexico
Hiking New York
Hiking North Carolina
Hiking the North Cascades
Hiking Northern Arizona
Hiking Olympic National Park
Hiking Oregon
Hiking Oregon's Eagle Cap Wilderness
Hiking Oregon's Mount Hood/Badger Creek
Hiking Oregon's Three Sisters Country
Hiking Pennsylvania
Hiking Shenandoah National Park
Hiking the Sierra Nevada
Hiking South Carolina
Hiking South Dakota's Black Hills Country
Hiking Southern New England
Hiking Tennessee
Hiking Texas
Hiking Utah
Hiking Utah's Summits
Hiking Vermont
Hiking Virginia
Hiking Washington
Hiking Wyoming
Hiking Wyoming's Cloud Peak Wilderness
Hiking Wyoming's Wind River Range
Hiking Yellowstone National Park
Hiking Zion & Bryce Canyon National Parks
The Trail Guide to Bob Marshall Country
Wild Country Companion
Wild Montana
Wild Utah

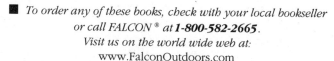

■ *To order any of these books, check with your local bookseller*
or call FALCON ® *at 1-800-582-2665.*
Visit us on the world wide web at:
www.FalconOutdoors.com

FALCON®

FALCON GUIDES ® Leading the Way

FIELD GUIDES

Bitterroot: Montana State Flower
Canyon Country Wildflowers
Central Rocky Mountains
   Wildflowers
Great Lakes Berry Book
New England Berry Book
Ozark Wildflowers
Pacific Northwest Berry Book
Plants of Arizona
Rare Plants of Colorado
Rocky Mountain Berry Book
Scats & Tracks of the Pacific
   Coast States
Scats & Tracks of the
   Rocky Mountains
Southern Rocky Mountain
   Wildflowers
Tallgrass Prairie Wildflowers
Western Trees
Wildflowers of Southwestern
   Utah
Willow Bark and Rosehips

FISHING GUIDES

Fishing Alaska
Fishing the Beartooths
Fishing Florida
Fishing Glacier National Park
Fishing Maine
Fishing Montana
Fishing Wyoming
Fishing Yellowstone
   National Park

ROCKHOUNDING GUIDES

Rockhounding Arizona
Rockhounding California
Rockhounding Colorado
Rockhounding Montana
Rockhounding Nevada
Rockhound's Guide to New
   Mexico
Rockhounding Texas
Rockhounding Utah
Rockhounding Wyoming

MORE GUIDEBOOKS

Backcountry Horseman's
   Guide to Washington
Camping California's
   National Forests
Exploring Canyonlands &
   Arches National Parks
Exploring Hawaii's Parklands
Exploring Mount Helena
Exploring Southern California
   Beaches
Recreation Guide to WA
   National Forests
Touring California & Nevada
   Hot Springs
Touring Colorado Hot Springs
Touring Montana & Wyoming
   Hot Springs
Trail Riding Western
   Montana
Wild Country Companion
Wilderness Directory
Wild Montana
Wild Utah

BIRDING GUIDES

Birding Minnesota
Birding Montana
Birding Northern California
Birding Texas
Birding Utah

PADDLING GUIDES

Floater's Guide to Colorado
Paddling Minnesota
Paddling Montana
Paddling Okefenokee
Paddling Oregon
Paddling Yellowstone & Grand
   Teton National Parks

HOW-TO GUIDES

Avalanche Aware
Backpacking Tips
Bear Aware
Desert Hiking Tips
Hiking with Dogs
Leave No Trace
Mountain Lion Alert
Reading Weather
Route Finding
Using GPS
Wilderness First Aid
Wilderness Survival

WALKING

Walking Colorado Springs
Walking Denver
Walking Portland
Walking St. Louis
Walking Virginia Beach

■ *To order any of these books, check with your local bookseller*
*or call FALCON ® at **1-800-582-2665**.*
Visit us on the world wide web at:
www.FalconOutdoors.com

FALCON®